Book One in the GRE/

LAUNCHING GREATER WORKS™

Turning a God-Inspired Vision Into a 501(c)(3) Nonprofit

SHERRYE WILLIS

Copyright © 2014 by Sherrye Willis

All rights reserved. This book is protected under the copyright laws of the United States of America, and may not be reproduced in any format without the written permission of the author.

ISBN-13: 978-1496151551

Printed in the United States of America

Cover Design and Interior Formatting: Steven C. Smith (designbysteven.com)

Unless otherwise noted, all scripture references are from the King James Version of the Holy Bible.

Scripture references notated as "ESV" are from (The Holy Bible, English Standard Version®) copyright © 2001 by Crossway, a publishing ministry of Good News Publishers. ESV® Text Edition: 2011. The ESV® text has been reproduced in cooperation with and by permission of Good News Publishers. Unauthorized reproduction of this publication is prohibited. All rights reserved.

Scripture notated as The Message Bible are taken from The Message. Copyright © 1993, 1994, 1995, 1996, 2000, 2001, 2002. Used by permission of NavPress Publishing Group.

Scripture taken from the NEW AMERICAN STANDARD BIBLE®, Copyright © 1960, 1962, 1963, 1968, 1971, 1972, 1973, 1975, 1977, 1995 by The Lockman Foundation. Used by permission.

DEDICATION

To my parents, the late Rev. Jeffrey and Annie Mae Ellison, who loved me unconditionally and planted in me the life I live today—I will always remember you.

To my husband and best friend, Joe—I am eternally grateful for your encouragement, support, and the sacrifices made for us to pursue the Alliance for Greater Works™ vision. Thank you for your love, servant leadership, and patience. I'll always love you.

To my sisters: Cathyrn, Patricia, Cathy, and my sister in-love since 12 years old—LaLoni (Lon)—Thank you for being my wind and always telling me I can do anything. I love you.

To my childhood church family—Johnson Memorial Church of God In Christ. I'll always cherish the biblical foundation provided and the life we lived out together. To my God-brother and -sister, Curtis and Mary, I'm thankful for the friendship we've shared since six years old.

To Dr. Cindy Shearer and David Yeazell, who coached me in writing this book. Thank you for your patience and diligently working to keep my heart and voice while editing.

Finally, to all those who offered me their time for interviews, advise and encouragement—Thanks! Candace Gray, Founding Board Member, Dallas, TX; Albert Martin, Founding Board Member, Lancaster, TX; Aaron Graham, Pastor of District Church, Washington, D.C.; Sarah Nelson and Monica Egert Smith, Communities Foundation of Texas, Dallas, TX; Dr. Maurice Pugh, Pastor of New Life Fellowship Church, Arlington, TX; Robert Triggs, Founder of Eternal Impact, Dallas, TX; Steve Vanderhill, Founder and President of Redeemer Seminary, Dallas, TX.

TABLE OF CONTENTS

Preface / 7

Book Format / 9

Introduction / 10

Part 1—Hearing and Answering the Service Call / 13

Chapter 1—In My Father's House / 15

Chapter 2—Toward a Purpose-Driven Life / 19

Chapter 3—Where I Started? / 23

Chapter 4—Stones of Remembrance / 27

Part 2—The Price and Process of Launching a 501(c)(3) / 31

Chapter 1—Start with Heart / 36

Chapter 2—Listen to Learn / 41

Chapter 3—Look Again and See the Need / 47

Chapter 4—Think Differently / 53

Chapter 5—Lead with a Voice of Vision / 62

Next Steps and Resources to Launch Greater Works™ / 67

Part 3—Alliance for Greater Works™ Overview / 69

About the Author / 70

Endnotes / 71

PREFACE

I wrote this book for four reasons. *First, I want those who have a vision planted in your heart to start a ministry or nonprofit to be able to achieve it.* Leaders who start a social service nonprofit, a social enterprise, or ministry often have the passion (heart) and calling to give hope and to restore people and the community to wholeness. But oftentimes, while visionaries have passion, they lack know-how, the practical skills, information and resources to achieve their vision.

Second, I want to keep you encouraged as you move forward in executing your vision. If you desire to start a nonprofit, but you don't know how, you can spend years going around in circles and never moving forward. You can feel like the children of Israel—who spent 40 years wandering around the same mountain, getting stuck— and never fully realize the greater works of your ministry. You could take one step forward and two steps backward. During the process, you, the visionary, can become very discouraged—feeling like you will never realize the vision that God birthed in your heart.

I hope by sharing my story that you will begin to recognize the journey that God has selected for you and the way that He has worked in your life to bring you to your place of purpose.

Third, I want you to understand the critical spiritual and administration skills needed to launch a ministry or nonprofit to greater works. Someone called to greater works needs both sets of skills. Those administrative skills include capacity for leadership, business skills, understanding of and articulation of message, and to be able to develop people. This book will help visionaries realize that you can grow your vision to reality when you engage your heart, ears, eyes, head and voice.

Fourth, I wrote this book to invite you to experience life at a deeper level by allowing your inner-self to guide and direct you not only in your spiritual life, but also your professional life. Trusting your life to Jesus Christ to achieve greater works in your life is an awesome experience. When Jesus walked this earth more than 2000 years ago, He called men and women to follow Him. When they experienced Him, their lives were transformed as they departed their old lifestyle and pursued the new pathway He had chosen.

The last 13 years has been my journey of following Him into new pathways. It has been a journey of successes with moments of discouragement (I have many) or uncertainties about the path. But, through the journey, I have seen what God can accomplish through a broken, yet willing vessel (I'll share more about this later in the book). And the best part is, I'm living my vision today!

BOOK FORMAT

This book is divided into two major sections. In the first section, I share my call and journey to start Alliance for Greater Works™ (formerly Faith & Philanthropy Institute). Part two introduces a greater works model that I have developed as a result of launching Alliance for Greater Works™ as well as working with other ministry and nonprofit leaders in realizing their visions.

Oftentimes, when visionaries begin to walk out their vision they don't stop to count the cost and assess their abilities as well as what is needed to accomplish it. They never think about the foundation required to build a strong ministry or nonprofit that has great impact. The model provides you a framework to launch greater works. Throughout the book, I share teachable moments from my journey that hopefully will benefit you in starting and growing a nonprofit or ministry.

I am prayerful that this book will lead you to strategic decisions for your God-inspired vision. With this book, it is my desire to help visionaries grow their ideas from good intentions to greater works.

INTRODUCTION

One of my favorite studies in Rick Warren's book *The Purpose-Driven Life* is day three, "What Drives Your Life." The study is a favorite because it mirrors my journey: humble beginnings with a strong foundation for a call that was overshadowed and driven by other issues as I entered my adult years—only to come full circle as I rediscovered and reconnected to God's purposes for my life.

Warren proposes that everyone is driven by something. Some people are driven by the need for love or to be successful. Some are driven by the guilt from something they did in the past or others did to them. Others may be driven by the acquisition of things, money, or approval. While there can be a momentary payoff in any of those areas that drive us, Warren communicates that ultimately drive for things all leads to the same dead end—unused potential, unnecessary stress, and an unfulfilled life. But, those who live a "purpose-driven life," a life guided, controlled, directed, and driven by God's purposes, understand what is really important—and experience meaning, focus, motivation, and simplicity in their lives.

Fortunately, there are many successful visionaries—men and women with a God-inspired vision, a call, and a good heart. They are men and women who glorify the Creator by making the world a better place for all through their work in the marketplace, ministry, nonprofit social service delivery or community development initiatives. They understand God's purposes, and live lives that are driven to see genuine and lasting transformation in our world.

To be God-inspired is important because I believe that we are spiritual beings living a human experience. Consequently the real meaning of life begins with knowing the true and living God. I've also come to understand that the vision of an organization succeeds when the leader's vision is God-inspired and guided by prayer like that of the biblical leader, Nehemiah.

I've seen how powerful vision and good works can be inspiring, but founding Alliance for Greater Works™ (formerly Faith & Philanthropy

Institute), I learned that a leader can be driven by a vision. To see that vision turned into a thriving, sustainable ministry or nonprofit—the greater works—a leader must have more than a good heart or a clear call. It also requires servant leadership, vision, strategy, human and financial capital, and a clear purpose.

WHAT IS A GOD-INSPIRED VISION?

A God-Inspired vision often starts with a crisis or a compelling need of human suffering. In the book of Nehemiah, the God-inspired vision was to restore the honor of the Jewish people, who were suffering from disgrace over the destruction of the walls surrounding Jerusalem—their spiritual and political capital. The destroyed walls left Jerusalem defenseless against their enemies, and the city had become a desolate ruin. Nehemiah's concern was a passionate response to the need.

In Nehemiah 1:1-3, Nehemiah received the report that the walls of Jerusalem were broken down and burned by fire, and that the remnant of Jews in the province was in great affliction and reproach. Nehemiah's initial response to the news revealed his concern for the people of God. With tears, he mourned, fasted and interceded in prayer before God for the people's sin, which led to their national shame.

Nehemiah's prayer for the defenseless condition of the people of God also reveals his concern for God's agenda. As Nehemiah pleaded the cause of the Jews, and mourned over their condition, he acknowledged the conditions of God's covenant with Israel—openly recognizing that God was right and the people had strayed from their part of the covenant. Nehemiah brings God into remembrance of His promise that if the people of Israel failed to keep the commandments of God they would be scattered, and conversely, if they obeyed God's commandments they would be gathered back to the place of promise.

As leaders, our heart concerns will be evident in the focus of our prayers. Do we only pray for our personal or family needs? Or has God placed in us the concern like Nehemiah felt for God's people and His agenda?

TRAITS OF A COMPELLING, GOD-INSPIRED VISION

A God-inspired vision begins with a relationship with God through His son Jesus Christ. When we accept the gift of Jesus Christ, we find our purpose. We cannot receive a God-inspired vision without knowing our purpose, and we do not have purpose without knowing God.

A compelling, God-inspired vision is usually based on needs beyond the ability and comfort-zone of the one called to lead the vision. A compelling vision will stretch the faith and dependence on God of the one called, so like the psalmist, they will say, "If it had not been for the Lord who was on our side..." (Psalm 124:1). Without God's help, there is little hope of success.

A compelling vision is fueled by the type of passion we see in Philippians 3:12 where Paul talks about counting all as loss to know Christ, be found in His righteousness, know Him and the power of His resurrection, and the fellowship of His sufferings. Paul said he had not already obtained it, or become perfect, but that he was "...forgetting those things which are behind, and reaching forth unto those things which are before, I press toward the mark for the prize of the high calling of God in Christ Jesus" (Phil. 3:13-14).

A compelling, God-inspired vision calls one to sacrifice in sweat, tears, possessions, and relationships.

In Nehemiah 2:1-3, we see that Nehemiah's concern for his people and the city of Jerusalem was still evident on his face four months following his receiving the initial news. Nehemiah put himself in a dangerous position by entering the king's presence in a state of sorrow. The king could execute anyone who displeased him. Nehemiah understood this danger. In verse two he states that he was afraid. Not only did his sorrow show in the king's presence, but when asked, he brought his personal concern to the king's attention. Nehemiah's concern for the condition of Jerusalem and his people overrode any concerns for his personal welfare. He risked failure, ridicule—and worse—by moving forward with the vision on his heart for a restored Jerusalem.

A compelling, God-inspired vision cannot be accomplished without the help of God and a myriad of other individuals: family, mentors, contacts, staff, and volunteers.

Nehemiah needed the favor of the king, the protection of the king's escort, and the Jews who joined him in rebuilding the wall. If every other individual or group of persons in this story had not been in its place, at the needed time, the project would not have been successful.

God prepares us for a compelling, God-inspired vision.

Your life experiences all add up to what you are uniquely fashioned for and called to. A compelling, God-inspired vision is not just a job or another ministry opportunity—it is a call that only you are uniquely tailored to fulfill.

A vision can be caught or discovered.

Mary, mother of Jesus, understood her purpose by revelation as the angel told her what was going to happen to her and her role in the vision's fulfillment. She "caught" the vision that she was uniquely selected to be the mother of the Messiah. Nehemiah understood his purpose and compelling vision by discovery as he responded to God and a pressing need through months of prayer, and research into the needs and size of the task he was called to address.

PART I
HEARING AND ANSWERING THE SERVICE CALL

"THE GREATEST AMONG YOU SHALL BE YOUR SERVANT."
(MATTHEW 23:11, ESV)

On February 16, 2001, God called me, and I was finally ready to listen. I awakened around 6:45 a.m. to begin my devotional/prayer time, still half asleep. As I had done many times before, I remember asking God what He wanted me to do with my life. As I sat still and in quietness, I heard a voice say "I want you to train leaders of faith in philanthropy, and the first training should be in September 2001." I remember the voice saying that the training should be "how to" and not a think-tank. Initially, I was afraid of the voice. But somehow I knew it was the voice of God speaking to me, and in time it gave me comfort.

At the time, I did not fully understand the God-inspired vision. But the voice assured me that if I was obedient and heeded the call, He would provide all the resources I needed to accomplish the call. I believed the direction was from God, and it somehow connected with my heart through the scriptures. I believe if you are willing to glorify God, by pursuing with all your heart what He has planted in your heart, God will honor your faith and bring it to pass.

My willingness to listen to the call of God that morning was the culmination of years of preparation. The call was charismatic in that God spoke to me and told me what He wanted me to do. But the call was also progressive. It was built on a foundation that was formed through the years I spent in my parents' house where they taught me to love God and serve humanity. And the foundation of expertise gained from years of professional experience. It all came together in that quiet morning in my bedroom when God challenged me to step out in a new direction of service.

THE TYPES OF CALL

There are three types of calls: (1) A call to redemption—God calls us all to be in relationship with Him; (2) a call to consecration—growing and devoting your whole self to God, and; (3) a call to service—God calls us to particular service that is based on our background, talent and experiences (see Luke 5). A service call is born out of a relationship with the Creator. In *Letters from the Desert*, Carretto provides a concise definition of a calling. He says,

God's call is mysterious; it comes in the darkness of faith. It is so fine, so subtle, that it is only with the deepest silence within us that we can hear it. And yet nothing is so decisive and overpowering for a man or woman on this earth, nothing surer or stronger. This call is uninterrupted: God is always calling us! But there are distinctive moments in this call of His, moments which leave a permanent mark on us—moments which we never forget.

Robert, youth pastor and founder of the ministry Eternal Impact, defines a calling as a burden to carry out a divine summons from God and/or to accomplish a task or responsibility to a certain group of people or a geographic area.

HOW THE CALL OCCURS

When one senses the call, it can occur in two different ways:
- A charismatic call: comes primarily through a spiritual encounter or revelation.
- A progressive call: develops over time as God deals with your heart, works through circumstances, and other people to confirm the call.

CHAPTER 1
IN MY FATHER'S HOUSE

My father and mother are my ultimate role models in the work I do today. Through their lives, my parents taught me that it's not what a person acquires in life that measures success, but what a person is willing to give to those around them. At three days old, my parents adopted me and gave me the gift of love, life, and a home filled with laughter and family.

I was raised in a small town called Corsicana, about 55 miles south of Dallas, Texas. It's a place where everyone knows your name. And everyone waves at and blows their horns at passersby as they drive down the street. In this rural community, even if they're not, everybody is your cousin—and your local church is considered your extended family.

My parents, Jeffrey and Annie Mae Ellison, were servant leaders who led by example. They taught me with their actions that I must choose to have a serving heart. My parents were willing to reach beyond themselves to serve and help others because their greatest desire was to live a life that brought glory and honor to God. They did not wait for others to help their neighbors. They committed their lives to caring for individuals that were broken, marginalized, and experiencing poverty in their world. Growing up we didn't have a lot of material things, but we were not poor in mind and were willing to share whatever we had with others.

My parents were well over 50 when I entered their world, but they were full of life and lifelong learners. Before starting elementary school, I remember attending school with them in the evenings where they both completed their GEDs. It was in these classes that I developed a love for learning and helping people to learn. Often I would join the class in learning new words and arithmetic. Other times, the teacher allowed me to help in the class by picking up homework assignments or cleaning the black boards. At home, my parents allowed me to help them with their homework. My parents always pushed me in academics and taught me that education is one of the keys to get out of poverty.

I also remember vividly on Sundays, Wednesdays, Fridays, and

Saturdays, my family traveled approximately seventy-five miles round trip from Corsicana to Athens, Texas to a rural community church where my father was the pastor. Oftentimes on the way home, my parents would pick up families we saw walking along the highway, welcome them into our home and table, to share a meal with us, clean clothes, a place for refreshment, and money to get them to their destination.

My father was also a farmer who taught me the importance of the simple things in life through his enjoyment of gardening and building things with his hands. In our backyard, we had a vegetable garden, chickens that hatched eggs, and a smokehouse to smoke the meat when one of our pigs was slaughtered. We also had pecan and fig trees. (Looking back, I realize how self-sufficient our lives were.)

In modern terminology, we would call my dad an entrepreneur. Because of his creativity and initiative, we had everything we needed for survival on our land, or within easy access. Dad taught me that we have everything we need within ourselves. He taught that we have a God-given creative ability to create whatever we need—and that our needs are not always met through a traditional job and a weekly paycheck.

As a young girl, I captured some of dad's entrepreneurial spirit. I took old Purex bottles, cut off the spouts, crocheted beautiful coverings for the outside, lined the inside with soft fabric, and created purses. I generated income out of discarded items and some scraps of fabric. The older ladies at church—the "church mothers"—were my best customers! They asked for purses in every crochet color—red, black, blue, and green.

My father also taught me that seeking first to understand is the most important quality of a leader. He was a very quiet person. In most conversations other people would do all the talking. Dad would attentively listen. When they finally finished speaking, he would repeat back to them a summary of what they had said and didn't say. As he listened to their words, he was also hearing their hearts.

My father enjoyed stillness. He spent many hours outside in nature, taking walks, or sitting reading. In the early morning, I often heard him outside reading his Bible and praying. He taught me that I need to be willing to be still and listen to God—personally, and as a leader, it is through stillness that I can hear God's direction.

My mother worked as a housekeeper and caretaker to children of professionals in the white community. She was a very warm and giving person who believed that the mark of a great leader starts with developing the inner-self. She taught me that I am a servant leader when I am willing to love others and give my best rather than seeking to always take. I learned that lesson practically when we had guests in the house.

My bedroom had a special appeal. It was situated in the front of the house with a big window that looked out to a beautiful rose tree. So whenever we had houseguests—missionaries, family, friends—I was the first asked to sacrifice my room and sleep elsewhere in the house. I didn't like that—I wanted my room. But my mom was teaching me the importance of sharing with others. Not only did I have to sacrifice my room, I had to share my clothes and other possessions with others in need. It wasn't an option. My parents required this. They wanted me to understand that what God had blessed me with was not just for my consumption, but for others in need.

My mom loved making children happy. Our house and yard was always filled with the neighborhood kids. Each morning she woke up before the crack of dawn to cook the best "tea-cakes" in the world for her family, and the neighborhood children. I can taste them even now. While walking me to kindergarten and elementary school in the mornings, she checked on the senior citizens in our neighborhood to ensure that they had what they needed. Oftentimes I saw my mother and father take senior citizens into our home and care for them if they didn't have family or could not care for themselves.

At age 12, I asked Jesus Christ to come into my heart. My parents were so excited! During summer Vacation Bible School, my church and neighborhood youth studied and memorized scriptures related to God's plan of salvation. We learned that we are all sinners because Romans 3:23 says that all have sinned and fall short of the glory of God.

Being a sinner means that we have all missed the mark. When we lie, hate, or hurt someone with our words, we have missed the standard God has set. We also learned that the penalty for sin is death. Romans 6:23 says, "For the wages of sin is death." In other words, by sinning we have earned death, meaning we deserve to die and be separated from God forever. But the Good News is that Christ died in the place of you and me! Romans 5:8

says, "...God shows his love for us in that while we were still sinners, Christ died for us" (ESV). I learned that I can be saved through faith in Christ (see Ephesians 2:8-9). Having faith means to trust. I must trust and depend on Christ alone to forgive me and to give me eternal life.

Our class even discussed that trusting Christ means more than going to church, being a good person or helping the poor. It means having a relationship with Jesus and asking Him to come into our hearts. I remember thinking I wanted Jesus to live in my heart and to guide me through life. I told my vacation Bible School teacher, Mrs. Lampkin, I wanted to be saved and she led the entire class through the sinner's prayer: "Dear God, I know I'm a sinner. I know my sin deserves to be punished. I believe that Jesus Christ died for me and rose from the grave. I trust Jesus Christ alone as my Savior. Thank you for the forgiveness and everlasting life I now have, in Jesus' name. Amen." You too can be saved if you pray to God and believe it in your heart.

At age 15, my father died. This was a devastating time for me because I was a daddy's girl. Our family church—Johnson Memorial Church—became my family's support system. They were there to strengthen my mom, sister Cathryn, and me, through the good and the bad. They shared their meals, financial resources, and special moments with my family—they showed me what it really means to love your neighbor as yourself. The greatest gift that they gave was the emphasis on developing a deep relationship with my heavenly Father and discerning His will for my life. I saw first-hand what it means to "do life together" with a church family. The Johnson Memorial Church family still holds a special place in my heart even today, including close relationships with the members from my generation. Many are now pastors, evangelists, teachers, psalmists, urban ministers, as well as business leaders in the marketplace.

Those formative years became the foundation that prepared me for the call that I experienced in 2001—the entrepreneurial spirit, the servant leadership heart, a willingness to sacrifice for others, the care for the community and the role of the church in the community. But most importantly, I learned to be willing to listen and hear the voice of God, and live life out of the inner core of that relationship with God.

CHAPTER 2
TOWARD A PURPOSE DRIVEN LIFE

Leaving small-town Corsicana, I moved to the big city, Dallas, to continue my education. With a two-year college degree, and administrative secretary work experience under my belt, I applied for and accepted a position as inside semiconductor sales person for General Electric. Within a couple years I was bored by the job and prayed, asking God what He wanted for me. I remember saying to Him, Lord if this is not it, please let me know. Three months after praying that prayer, I had a partial answer. GE and RCA merged, and I was laid off from my job.

Due to the economy at the time, I could not find work. I was not seeking for a job in the nonprofit world, but the first position that opened for me was as a receptionist at a nonprofit organization. Not only was the position a lesser role, but also the pay—a more than 50% reduction. But God's provision sustained me. Three months later I was promoted to administrative assistant. Three months after that I was asked to help start the Nonprofit Loan Fund at the Center for Nonprofit Management. That was the beginning of what became 15 years working in large nonprofit institutions such as the Dallas Symphony Association and Dallas Museum of Art in key areas like fundraising—where I helped raise $3+ million annually.

While I enjoyed my positions and the knowledge I gained, I recognized that my real passion was working with grassroots organizations serving under-resourced communities. I felt that if those organizations that were making a difference in the lives of the poor and needy had the resources that the symphony and museum had, we would see real transformation in our communities.

In 1998, I became Senior Director of Development in a team that was pioneering the first Rising Star Scholarship program, which provided two years of free college education to any student in Dallas County who desired to go to college but could not afford it.

I was excited about this opportunity. My role on the team was to work closely with the Executive Director and Board Chairman of the Dallas Community College District Foundation to design and implement a $32 million endowment campaign. The interest from the endowment principal would yield the annual resources to allow students to receive tuition, books, and fees if they had a "B" average or above.

Creating something "out of the box" was stimulating and exciting, but the process in building the program strategy was stressful. There was a lot of excitement and support amongst Dallas philanthropists, businesses and foundations for the program. The Rising Star team raised nearly $20 million in 18 months.

Through that experience I learned that anytime you're creating something new, you always do more than you originally signed up for. With all of the physical stress from the project development and fundraising, I begin to experience health issues. As I neared twenty-four months, I began to ask God if this was really what I should be doing for the rest of my life.

By September 2000, I was at a crossroads in my life. It was the culmination of many things. From 1992-1998, I went through a career phase where I couldn't do anything right. It seemed like everything I touched was filled with conflict and drama. I wanted to get out of the nonprofit sector, but every door for employment that opened was in the nonprofit sector. I was tired of the constant disagreements with leadership, and began to look inward to see what was wrong with me.

I was at a point of emotional and spiritual brokenness. My work life was affecting my health, peace of mind, and my personal relationships. One day, I stayed home from the office and spent the day in prayer. I cried out to God to help me understand what was happening in my life. As He revealed my issues, I asked Him to replace what I saw as my selfish, stony heart with His heart and desires for my life. To create in me a heart that is giving, serving, and responsive to Him—all the things I had learned from my parents and church.

Through prayer and studying God's Word, I began to see a clearer vision of His purpose for my life. One of my light-bulb moments in this process was reading Matthew 6:33:

"What I'm trying to do here is to get you to relax, to not be so preoccupied with getting, so you can respond to God's giving. People who don't know God and the way He works fuss over these things, but you know both God and how He works. Steep your life in God-reality, God-initiative, and God-provision. Don't worry about missing out. You'll find all your everyday human concerns will be met."

(The Message Bible)

I realized in that moment my priority should be to be driven by the things that honor God's values, and I should live according to His economy. My life had slipped off the foundation that my parents laid. I was being driven by success and money and was suffering for it. And God was dealing with me to leave my full-time position and step out in a direction that was more aligned with my purpose and call in life.

Out of this desire to live a purpose-driven life, I decided to change my career focus. I knew He was telling me it was time to leave my full-time job—something that was neither comfortable nor easy for me to consider. But I knew I had to do what He said even though it would stretch me. I shared with my husband, Joe, that it was time for me to launch out on my own. He was shocked. Our household was not accustomed to only one income. Joe urged us to pray about it, and that if God provided a part-time opportunity for me, we would consider the change.

One day, in early October 2000, as I was riding the train home, I had a strong impression to call Heather. I felt that I should let her know that I was possibly leaving my full-time position, and ask if she had any opportunities at her private foundation. Heather is a dear person that I became friends with while working at the Dallas Museum of Art. She and I always joked about me one day running her family's private foundation that gives nearly $500,000 annually in grants to nonprofits encouraging academic excellence in under-resourced communities. The day I called her she responded excitedly, "Are you serious!?" She wanted to know my salary requirement, and set an appointment to meet.

Meeting Heather and her sister-in-law, Jenny, I told them that I felt that I was moving in a new direction, and I desired to work part-time to focus my efforts on following my passion. Within a couple of days, Heather called me back and asked me when I could start.

On January 5, 2001, I left the Senior Director of Development position, started as part-time Executive Director of the Esping Family Foundation, and started my own nonprofit consulting business—Willis Partners Consulting—providing grant writing services to small grassroots organizations.

It was then, only a few short weeks later, that I received the call from God to train leaders in faith and philanthropy at a September 2001 event. About two weeks after the call from God, I was inundated with telephone calls from churches and faith-based organizations informing me that President George W. Bush had announced his White House Office of Faith-Based and Community Initiatives, whose purpose was to help promote public/private partnerships to enable diverse sacred places and grassroots secular programs to achieve civic purposes. The leaders calling wanted help to "get some of the funds," but they didn't know how to write a grant or begin the process. Through an assessment of the organizations, I quickly realized that many lacked the capacity to apply for or use grants effectively.

CHAPTER 3
WHERE I STARTED?

The journey to accomplish the directive started with self. I had to first assess myself to see if I was prepared. Any time you want to lead, you have to know your strengths and weaknesses. I spoke to my dear friend and mentor, Curtis Meadows, who said that I needed to know what kind of personality I had and had to prepare for the role I was called for. Was I a Moses (the main, out front, leader) or an Aaron (a support for a leader, who is the voice of the leader)? Curtis was essentially saying that I needed to know myself. He also said I needed to become disciplined in my mind, will and emotions. That I needed to be mature as a leader—not all over the place—because a leader does not lead just for themselves, but in the service of others.

There were days and nights after the call was planted in my heart that I felt inept, overwhelmed, and incapable to carry out the directive. I prayed many times asking God to show me what to do, who I should talk to, and what were the first steps. I begin by researching what was currently taking place locally and nationally in the direction that I was being led. I also talked to national leaders to learn about the current work. As I researched and explored the situation in the Dallas community and around the country, I gained a greater insight into the work. With this information and constant prayer, I developed an outline of the three-day intensive program that we would offer on September 26-28 in Dallas, Texas.

I named the initiative Faith & Philanthropy because these were the two words that I heard the morning I received the initial call. *Faith* related to the faith community that was the target audience, and *philanthropy* because the goal was to connect the leaders' and organizations' love for mankind to the necessary funding resources. (Many individuals view philanthropy as money, but the root word *phileo*, means brotherly love, and, a love for mankind.)

SHARING THE VISION WITH OTHERS

In March 2001, I took the program outline and shared it with two people whom I admire greatly—Candace Gray, Program Director at the Foundation for Community Empowerment at the time, and, Albert Martin, a pastor and director of the southwest region's Fannie Mae Foundation. Over lunch, I communicated with them my directive and the program that I wanted to offer in September 2001. Excitedly, they became the first two supporters of the vision outside of immediate family.

When I spoke with Candace recently about our work 13 years ago, she recalled it was a needed vision, but she immediately knew there were challenges. There was already a lot of talk by various people about doing capacity building. She felt we would definitely have to communicate and educate others on the distinctiveness of Alliance for Greater Works™ (formerly Faith & Philanthropy Institute) because of the then launch of the White House Office of Faith-Based and Community Initiatives. She noted that the September date was approaching quickly. But also saw that a lot of pieces were coming together as God orchestrated speakers for the event. Reflecting on the past helped us to realize that God was with us then and He is with us today.

The morning I shared the vision with Albert Martin, he felt a leaping in his heart because he knew it was from God. He saw it as a way to connect the church world to the giving community. That would allow ministries to grow and develop leadership to acquire the business acumen that they did not receive in a seminary setting. Albert remembered the planning journey and the partners we engaged to accomplish the work, and the sense of urgency to do it regardless of what we thought or felt. It was like a birthing process. It had started, and it was growing day by day. Either we would birth it or die.

The three of us developed a list of individuals and organizations that we wanted to be a part of the September 2001 program. The next three months we met with business leaders, pastors, nonprofit leaders, universities/seminaries, government, and individuals to share the vision and ask them to be a part of the initiative: serve as advisors, provide financial support and/or share the program with their constituencies.

WORKING THE PLAN

In June 2001, I partnered with the Foundation for Community Empowerment to organize a focus group of faith leaders to better understand the challenges they faced in effectively operating their community initiatives. There were pastors from both the southern and northern sector of Dallas in attendance. We discovered they needed the know-how and support to build programs and develop community development corporations (CDC) to manage and fund the programs. How to lead a CDC, partnering with the funding community, writing a case for support, measuring impact and outcomes and developing a strategic business plan were among the areas of need.

What we gleaned from that landmark gathering remains the foundation from which many of the current Alliance for Greater Works™ (formerly Faith & Philanthropy Institute) programs and services are based. As a result of the focus group, a planning committee was formed to plan the first Institute at the Loews Anatole Hotel.

By August, the speakers were identified, location confirmed, and brochure printed and mailed. With the assistance of the planning committee our keynote speakers included:

- Rev. Dr. James Joseph, South African Ambassador and first African American President of the Council on Foundations
- Dr. Ray Bakke, Bakke Graduate University
- Dr. Fred Lucas, The Faith Center, New York
- Stephen Lazarus, Center for Public Justice, Washington, D.C.

With the date, location and speakers in place, the 2001 Moving Beyond the Walls conference was marketed throughout the southwest region of the U.S.

My devotionals during the month of August all seemed to have one theme—"obedience is better than sacrifice." Many times God asks us to do one thing, and instead of doing that thing we do something else. God is not impressed with what we sacrifice to do something He hasn't called us to do. He is looking for obedience to His plan. One morning I read about King Saul, who had been instructed by God to handle things in one way, but He chose to do it another way. I didn't understand what God was trying to tell me through my devotions. I remember closing my Bible and crying out to God, saying "Father, am I not doing what you asked me to do? I don't understand. Am I being disobedient?" I did not get an immediate answer.

THE TOWERS FALL

Before September 11, 2001, there were very few registrants for the three-day conference. And the events of that fatal day literally stopped our country. With the nation in crisis, I returned to prayer asking God what I should do about the conference. He responded to me by saying, "I knew what would happen in September when I told you to do this in February 2001. Be obedient!"

Several days after 9/11, the Alliance for Greater Works™ (formerly Faith & Philanthropy Institute) planning committee met to assess where we were and our next steps. I reported to the committee that we had very few registrants. As I outlined the current status, several of the members of the committee recommended that we postpone the conference until March 2002, explaining that people were afraid to travel and this would be an excellent reason to reschedule.

As I sat there and listened to the explanation for not doing the program, I realized that this was what my earlier devotional on obedience was preparing me for. I allowed them to complete their presentation of why we should postpone the program. When they finished, I shared with the committee that this was more than an idea, but a call from God, so I had to do what I was commanded to do by Him.

I shared that I too was concerned about the attendance and the fact that we had received more than $75,000 in funding for this program. But I knew this was something we had to do even if it was only the committee members and the less than 25 attendees registered in attendance. I also shared with them that as people of faith, the need for spiritual renewal and outreach to the community was particularly pivotal during that time of uncertainty and unrest. The alliance agreed and rallied around the program with renewed energy.

The committee got on the telephone and shared with people about the conference. We continued to market the program on radio, television, and in the newspapers. On September 26-28, 2001, there were over 125 attendees who participated: leaders from Arkansas, Louisiana, Oklahoma, and Texas. We were the only program to offer an event in the Loews Anatole of Dallas during that week and had the entire hotel to ourselves for the entire three days.

On the second day of the training program, as Dr. Fred Lucas of New York, NY was speaking during lunch, a woman and her two friends, also from New York, NY, showed up at the entrance of the banquet room. The ladies saw the hotel from the freeway. One of the ladies in the car told her friends to stop. She had seen the hotel building in a dream seven days before and seven years before. She said that God told her if she would find this place she would find the answer to her dreams. When she found us in the hotel, she said that God told her to tell us that this initiative will go to the nations.

CHAPTER 4
STONES OF REMEMBRANCE

Since our launch in September 2001, we have trained and influenced multiple organizations, communities, and leaders. And, as the woman from New York shared, we have gone to the nations. As I reflect back on the first 13 years as an organization, there are "twelve stones of remembrance" that we have been given. The idea of stones of remembrance comes from Joshua 4:20-22, where Joshua—after Israel crossed the Jordan River on dry ground—took 12 stones out of the Jordan and set them up at Gilgal as a memorial of what God had done. Joshua said to the Israelites that "When your children ask their fathers in times to come, 'What do these stones mean?' then you shall let your children know, 'Israel passed over this Jordan on dry ground'" (ESV).

STONE #1—PURPOSE
The original vision for Faith & Philanthropy Institute, from February 16, 2001, was defined as bringing together diverse sectors of community including faith, philanthropy, neighborhood leaders, business, and government to transform under-resourced communities. In January 2014, Faith & Philanthropy Institute's name was changed to Alliance for Greater Works™ to better depict our mission.

STONE #2—PIONEERING
In 2003, Alliance for Greater Works™ was selected to serve in Texas' FIRST White House for Faith-based and Community Initiatives grant as the Foundation for Community Empowerment's capacity building partner. Alliance for Greater Works™ designed and implemented the three-year program called Building Capacity, Building Communities. The program equipped more than 125 organizations in low-income communities throughout the city of Dallas with intensive training/coaching and assisted in distributing over $1.3 million in sub-grants to Dallas faith-based and community, grassroots organizations. As a result of this program, the organizations have since increased their net worth in excess of $10 million.

STONE #3—PLATFORM (INTERNATIONAL)
In 2006, Dr. Tony Evans introduced the National Church Adopt-A-School Initiative (NCAASI)—modeled after his church's successful Project Turn-Around program around church-school partnerships. Alliance for Greater Works™ equipped and partnered with Dr. Evans and his national ministry, The Urban Alternative, to implement the NCAASI program, as well as provide technical assistance to churches across the country as they implemented the program in their communities. Today, the NCAASI program has trained over 2,000 leaders in the U.S., Guam, Haiti, Mexico, and Bahamas.

STONE #4—PARTNERSHIPS
From 2006 through 2010, Alliance for Greater Works™ participated in formal collaborations with the Dallas Leadership Foundation executing grants from the Department of Health and Human Services and Department of Justice to train and equip faith-based and community leaders serving low-income communities throughout the city of Dallas. One of the programs was a three-year project called Communities Empowering Youth. The participating leaders strengthened their organizations and their service delivery in the areas of operational effectiveness, financial sustainability, human capital development and strategic collaborations. In addition, they increased their funding to nearly $890K, the number of youth in Dallas served to nearly 7,400, and affected a multi-million dollar ROI on the original $1 million grant award.

STONE #5—PACESETTER
Recognizing the need of religious organizations to increase their financial accountability and better understand the legal and ethical implications of their actions, in 2007, Alliance for Greater Works™ joined forces with accounting firms, Sommerville & Associates, P.C., Ratliff & Associates, P.C. and legal firm, Weycer, Kaplan, Pulaski, and Zuber, P.C., to annually host the Ultimate Financial and Legal Conference™. This event hails participants from across the U.S.—as far as Seattle on the West Coast and Washington, D.C. on the East Coast. Over 800 leaders have been served since the inception of this program, and 2014 will mark the 8th year for the conference.

STONE #6—PROGRESS
Because of Alliance for Greater Works™ impact working with North Texas faith-based organizations, our reach extended to Missouri through a partnership with the Nonprofit Services Consortium of St. Louis, MO. Alliance for Greater Works™ designed and presented a customized program on building a fundable, faith-based organization and trained over 100 organizations across the state.

STONE #7—PERFORMANCE STANDARDS FOR THE SECTOR
After a successful pilot program that ran from May 2009-January 2010, Alliance for Greater Works™ held its first full nine-month Master Nonprofit Consultant Certificate Program to train consultants to effectively and ethically use their expertise and experiences to assist nonprofit organizations in achieving their missions. As well, participants learned the basics of professional coaching and completed a comprehensive business plan for their own consulting business. After completing the course, one of the consultants went on to garner sales of over $200,000 in less than one year.

STONE #8—PROMOTING THE POWER OF COLLABORATION
Also in 2009, Alliance for Greater Works™ introduced the IGNITE Greater Works™ Gathering, designed to celebrate, equip and inform the community of the most effective faith-based, best-practice collaborative program models in Dallas, as well as to "ignite" a greater passion for community outreach and development among churches, nonprofits, funders and individuals. The inaugural event was held in collaboration with the Dallas Justice Revival sponsored by Sojourners. Over 250 people participated and 10 Dallas ministries were recognized and awarded for their work and for creating best-practice program models with measurable community impact in the areas of affordable housing, positive youth development, formerly incarcerated re-entry, poverty/homelessness, community collaboration and more. More than 25 collaborations between faith-based and community organizations occurred as a result this initiative.

STONE #9—PEOPLE
People are the greatest asset of an organization because they are the hands and feet utilized to fulfill the mission. Alliance for Greater Works™ is grateful for all the right people at the right time, including the founding Board of Directors, current board, volunteers, consultant network, staff, as well as the financial investors over the last thirteen years.

STONE #10—PROVIDENCE
In September 2001, it was confirmed that Alliance for Greater Works™ vision would go to the nations. Providentially, February 2011 and February 2013, we experienced the unfolding of this confirmation as we provided intensive training seminars to faith leaders on the island of Bermuda.

STONE #11—POSITIONING
In 2012, I was honored to be one of 150 U. S. leaders invited from across the country to the White House to gather alongside administration officials to discuss the challenges faced in local cities. The goal was to learn from pioneers who are driving change in challenging times and to explore new ways federal policymaking can support their endeavors. Only three Texas organizations were invited.

STONE #12—PRIORITIES
In 2013, Alliance for Greater Works™ brought attention to the important role women play in community development. On May 2, 2013, we introduced the Women Leading Greater Good™ Forum and convened more than 100 extraordinary women leaders in nonprofit, philanthropy, government, and business sectors working to advance solutions to today's tough social issues. Twelve women pioneers from the business, nonprofit, and philanthropy sectors were honored for their contributions to community development. As a result of the 2013 Forum, Alliance for Greater Works™ will allocate a large percentage of its resources to implement a Multicultural Women Initiative (MWI), the first of its kind in the Southern Region of the U.S. The purpose of this initiative is to create a space where a new generation of women of color business, faith, and social innovators/leaders can be identified and nurtured.

God places us in unique families, jobs and personal experiences to prepare us for our ultimate purpose. The work of Alliance for Greater Works™ started with a heart to honor God fully with my whole self. The greater works came as a result of abandoning my selfish desires and being willing to exchange my selfish life for the original design that God desired for me. As I stepped away from being a self-leader, driven by pride and what ultimately benefits me—I was able to step into a new sense of purpose in my life call.

PART 2
THE PRICE AND PROCESS OF LAUNCHING A 501(C)(3)

Launching a 501(c)(3) nonprofit is a serious and rigorous task. A common perception is that the nonprofit world is simply about doing good works, and that unlimited charitable support is available. That perception has led many to believe that starting and growing a 501(c)(3) is effortlessly achieved within one or two years. It simply does not happen that way. The reality is that of the over 1.6 million U.S. nonprofits (including ministries), 84% of those nonprofit organizations are unsustainable according to the *2011 Daring to Lead Executive Leadership study*. That means that many nonprofits and ministries in our communities cannot achieve their intended purpose because they don't have the capital, including money, staff, investors, and volunteers.

If you are a visionary beginning the process of launching a nonprofit, you must first count the cost and clearly understand why you are starting a new organization. The assessment must consider more than your passion for the cause. You might think that if you live out your passion as the leader, others will handle the work. While people will hopefully come to support and assist you, the reality is there is no substitute for your ability to lead, administer, and execute the necessary processes and requirements to start, manage, and grow a 501(c)(3) nonprofit.

As a visionary, you must ask the hard questions before launching a nonprofit: What type of a leader are you? Do you have the business intelligence and bandwidth for the task?

THE BALANCING ACT—SERVANT LEADERSHIP

The process of launching a nonprofit organization requires a balancing act by the visionary. The founder must be a servant while also having strong business intelligence. As a servant leader, the founder sees leadership as an act of service and not self-promotion or negative EGO

(Edging God Out) but rather healthy EGO (Exalting God Only) through their work.[1] This sounds easy on paper, but to walk out exalting God without elevating yourself requires letting God peel off all the layers of pride and self-centeredness that we all contain. This process is a journey of surrender. By surrendering your will and direction to God you become clearer of your purpose here on earth—to glorify God with your time, talents, and treasures.

My journey of founding Alliance for Greater Works™, outlined in the first half of this book, occurred over a seven-month period of time. But the lessons learned and God's hand in maturing me as a person and as a leader has taken more than thirteen years. And, I continue to grow as I yield to the Holy Spirit. While it may or may not take you less, more or the same amount of time to grow your vision, it's important to understand that the journey is not overnight.

Many people refer to themselves as a servant leader, but they still function as self-leaders. As a self-leader, they spend most of their time protecting their status rather than mastering pride and fear. They are very protective of themselves at work and often hide behind positions, withhold information, intimidate others, become competitive control freaks. While from birth we all start as self-serving people, we must be willing to grow and mature as an adult and realize that life is not about what we can get, but rather what we give.[2]

Being a servant leader is a strong and powerful example for living, because a servant-leader is a servant first and leader second. It begins with the desire to serve others. Then conscious choice brings one to aspire to lead. The best test to determine true servant leadership is to ask the following questions: Do those served grow as persons? Do they, while being served, become healthier, wiser, freer, more autonomous, more likely themselves to become servants? And, what is the effect on the least privileged in society? Will they benefit, or, are they left even more destitute?

THE BALANCING ACT—BUSINESS INTELLIGENCE

The other side of the balancing act is that a founder must possess business intelligence. Business intelligence is the ability to identify, dig-out, and analyze the facts of a situation. Business intelligence is necessary in developing a nonprofit business model clearly outlining a process by which your nonprofit delivers programs and services to the community while generating revenue to sustain the mission.

I have often heard nonprofit and ministry leaders say they do not need a business model or plan of action. Their reasons are that they are not a commercial enterprise and prefer to be led by God, or allow their creativity to lead. They believe that by having a business plan, they are not trusting God, or they will be restricted in moving forward with their vision.

I strongly believe in the power of God's leading and the process of strategic planning. From my point of view, trusting God and planning are interconnected. One of God's first actions in the world was to create structure and order out of chaos. He created the structure of heaven and earth and organized the day from the night. He put form where there was no form. By developing a plan for your nonprofit, you are allowing your God-ordained abilities to turn ideas (chaos) into an order.

Strategic planning is strategic because it involves a process preparing the best way to respond to the conditions of the organization's environment. Nonprofits often must respond to dynamic and even hostile environments. The strategic process is about planning because it involves intentionally setting goals (i.e., choosing a desired future) and developing an approach to achieving those goals. The process is disciplined in that it calls for a certain order and pattern to keep it focused and productive. Finally, the process is about fundamental decisions and actions because choices must be made in order to answer the sequence of questions mentioned above.

Strategic planning is an act of stewardship because the primary purpose is to help an organization do a better job of:
- Focusing its resources;
- Ensuring that members of the organization are working toward the same goals;
- Assessing and adjusting the organization's direction in response to a changing environment.

In short, strategic planning is a disciplined effort to produce fundamental decisions and actions that shape and guide what an organization is, what it does, and why it does it, with a focus on the future.[3] Note, there is still room for God's leading before, during, and after the planning process.

THE BANDWIDTH FOR THE TASK

In addition to business intelligence, the visionary must also have the bandwidth—capacity—to build diverse, strategic relationships that stretch and challenge them in their leadership and knowledge. Many times I have made the mistake of staying in my office and not taking the initiative to meet with key stakeholders. And for that, I have paid the price of people not knowing about the work that Alliance for Greater Works™ provides. As a visionary leader, it is critical to build social networks across all sectors. Strategic relationships are critical for your growth and the organization's growth.

At the end of the day, the founder must be willing to make many personal and professional sacrifices. The reality is that to establish a strong and thriving nonprofit ministry, you must be prepared to spend a lot of hours in prayer (isolated). You must also spend many hours reading, learning, and understanding the current situation of your target audience priorities. And then decide how to develop innovative solutions to address those priorities. It also requires having the discipline to consistently share your vision with key stakeholders.

Over the next five chapters, I will draw from my experience of founding Alliance for Greater Works™, with a focus on the business side of launching greater works. The last thirteen-years have taught me key practices that have helped me to turn a God-inspired vision into a 501(c)(3) nonprofit. The five key practices are: (1) Start with Heart; (2) Listen to Learn; (3) Look Again and See the Need; (4) Think Differently, and; (5) Lead with a Voice of Vision.

DEMYSTIFYING THE NONPROFIT SECTOR?

The nonprofit sector, often referred to as the third sector or social sector, is made up of approximately 1.6 nonprofits, foundations, and religious congregations benefitting the overall welfare of our society. A group interested in obtaining a 501(c)(3) tax-exempt status secures the designation from the Internal Revenue Service (IRS). To become a 501(c)(3) nonprofit, the organization's purpose must benefit the broad public interest and not just the members of the organization. In addition, the nonprofit's purpose must be charitable, religious, educational, scientific, literary, testing for public safety, fostering national or international amateur sports competition, and/or the prevention of cruelty to children or animals.

In my 25 years of working in and with the nonprofit sector, the two questions that I am asked most often from visionary leaders are:
(1) Do nonprofit staff receive a salary and benefits? (2) Can a nonprofit make a profit? The answer is yes to both questions. Staff in nonprofits can and do receive salary and benefits based on the position and the size of the nonprofit's annual operating budget. A nonprofit is a business and must have human capital to fulfill its mission.

In addition, a nonprofit is not only permitted to earn profits but should actively pursue achieving a profit at the end of the year. The difference between the for-profit and nonprofit sector is how the profit is used. In the nonprofit sector, the profit can be placed in the nonprofit's reserves and/or used to expand the programs rather than distributed as dividends for its board and investors. The 501(c)(3) tax-exempt status is a designation that allows the organization to be exempt from federal income taxation. It is not a self-fulfilling prophecy of "no" profit.

CHAPTER 1
START WITH HEART

"Because God has made us for Himself, our hearts are restless until they rest in Him." ~ Augustine of Hippo

The human heart is a fist-sized muscle that determines if we live or die—and affects the quality of life we have while alive. It pumps the blood that carries the vital nutrients and oxygen that our bodies need to function, and carries away waste products. If the heart stops—life stops! Similarly, if the heart is unhealthy, it negatively affects all the organs of our body, and hinders their ability to fulfill their individual roles.

Similar to all the muscles in our body, the heart contracts and expands. But, while our skeletal muscles will contract based on the level of resistance they meet at any given time, our heart contracts with all its force, an average of 72 times per minute for all the years of our allotted life. During an average human lifespan, this amazing muscle-pump contracts an estimated 2.5 billion times, sending 180 million liters of blood rushing through our body!

Our physical hearts deliver blood to our organs through the arteries. As our cells absorb the blood-rich nutrients and oxygen, the metabolic wastes and carbon dioxide that results is carried by the blood, through the veins, back to the heart—where the blood is cleaned. This deoxygenated blood is re-oxygenated and pumped back to the organs—in an uninterrupted cycle.

When the heart is healthy, the brain gets the oxygen and glucose that causes it to remain conscious. Our muscles receive the same, plus amino acids, and the proper combination of sodium, calcium, and potassium salts which allow them to contract normally. And the glands get a bountiful supply of raw materials which they use to create specific secretions. The organism that is the human body is dependent on the heart.

EXAMINING FIRST YOUR OWN "HEART"

Among the Webster's dictionary definitions for heart is the one I described above—the organ in our chest that pumps blood through our veins and arteries. But a second significant definition focuses on the heart as a person's innermost character or emotional and moral nature.[4] The idea is that we each have a physical heart-pump that is at the center core of our physical being, and also have a "heart" that is emotional and moral in nature and is at the core of our personality.

The Bible has much to say about the second definition. Proverbs 4:23 says, "Watch over your heart with all diligence, for from it *flow* the springs of life" (NASB). Other versions translate it as the "issues" of life. The idea is that all the issues of life originate in the heart—the innermost character of an individual—and flow out affecting all the other areas of a life.

Watching over the heart is crucial as what flows out of the heart will affect the words one speaks and one's actions. And similar to a human heart, which affects the quality of a physical life, what is pumped out of the innermost place of our moral and emotional nature affects not only our lives but the lives of those we interact with—positively or negatively.

A leader with perversity in his/her heart is said to continually devise evil—the result being actions and words that spread strife (Prov. 6:14). In my work history, I've had leaders who planned schemes for me to fail or would keep drama going in the organization by discussing an issue with everyone except the persons involved. I remember a manager that I reported to bullied people to manipulate them into doing what she wanted the subordinates to do. She once told me I was not smart and very disorganized. At the time, I was devastated. But later, as I thought about her words, I was reminded that administration and organizing are my strongest skills.

Along with perversity, those who devise evil are said to have deceit in their hearts (Prov. 12:20), and out of the mouth of a foolish heart comes folly and babbling (Prov. 12:23, 10:8). On the positive side, a tranquil heart is life to the body (Prov. 14:30) and wisdom rests in the heart of one who has understanding (Prov. 14:33). Have you ever stopped and asked yourself who you are at the core? Do you lead with perversity or peace?

Matthew 15:18 says, it is the things that proceed out of the mouth that come from the heart, and defile a person. Matthew goes on to say that "...out of the heart come evil thoughts, murders, adulteries, fornications, thefts, false witness, slanders" (Matt. 15:19, NASB).

Matthew also connects the relation of outward actions to the heart when he says, "...where your treasure is, there your heart will be also." Meaning, that the treasure—things you invest your time and money into—are a reflection of your heart. I have found that leaders who are sick and hurting in their own heart are those that hurt and destroy other people.

If you want to know the condition of your heart; look at what comes out of your life in speech and actions. "The good person out of the good treasure of his heart brings forth what is good; and the evil person out of the evil treasure brings forth what is evil; for their mouth speaks from that which fills his or her heart" (Luke 6:45, NASB). On the other hand, if you want to understand what kind of a person I am, look at my heart: "As in water face reflects face, so the heart of man reflects man" (Prov. 27:19, NASB).

Your heart becomes your compass for life and guides you to seek for those things that are pure, excellent, and honorable.

YOUR HEART IN RELATIONSHIP TO LAUNCHING A 501(C)(3)

As a leader contemplating the launch of a 501 (c)(3), the state of your heart will determine your success or failure in your venture. Are your motives based on a sincere desire to meet a societal need? Or are you launching your organization for self-benefit? The motives for starting a nonprofit or ministry can vary greatly. Some persons think there are endless opportunities to secure charitable contributions—and to pay themselves a healthy salary. Others may start a nonprofit to be socially correct or accepted in high profile spheres of influence.

But the driving force for those who desire to be a part of something greater is to create a new nonprofit ministry or venture because it's a heart matter. It is through our heart—that innermost core of our personality—that God speaks to us about a problem or need in society, just as He did to Nehemiah.

Returning from Jerusalem, Nehemiah's brother, Hanani, was anxious to share with his brother what he observed. Hanani explained that the people of Jerusalem were distressed and embarrassed because the walls of the city were broken down, and the gates were burned with fire. When Nehemiah heard this news, he wept.

When I first read the story of Nehemiah, I couldn't imagine why he cried because of the destroyed walls. The walls of Jerusalem had been down for 150 years—the news of their destruction was not new news, nor a surprise. But after meditating over that passage, I had the revelation that Nehemiah's weeping was a result of the Spirit of God touching his heart. Nehemiah's heart response to the news became the inner source that drove the outer activity that solved the problem. It is the same for us. Our heart drives the outer activity—the programs we administer, or nonprofit organizations we create—that we generate to solve the problem. Our nonprofit ministry to the community cannot just be a set of services we provide, or activities we generate to meet human need—our ministry must be a heartfelt response as an act of worship and obedience to God.

In my personal experience, the heart was the origin where the purpose of Alliance for Greater Works™ was birthed. And despite changes in the programs offered, and the way services are delivered over the years, the heart continues to be the motivator for all I do.

Similarly to our physical bodies, if the heart of a leader and their vision is healthy, the organization will be healthy. If the proper nutrients are getting to each functioning organ—each person in the organization—the organization can grow and expand and will be strengthened for the tasks it is called to perform.

But where the heart of the leader and their organization is unhealthy, the inner disease, while often not initially recognized by outsiders, will eventually flow out into each individual, department or program administered in the organization. And the biblical principle holds true that what is on the outside will quickly reflect what is in the heart, and the organization will suffer, the individuals and outreach will atrophy, and the organization will eventually die.

GETTING IN TOUCH WITH YOUR HEART

If you are having a difficult time getting in touch with your heart and connecting what is in your heart to what you are called to do—look at the following five elements:

First, look to scripture. What does scripture tell you about your role in the world around you? What does God call you to and require of you? And, how are your actions in the world a reflection of your faith?

Second, analyze your context. What are the needs of and dynamics within your community (we will discuss this more in a later chapter)? What do you see in your local community that tugs at your heart—and compels you to find a solution to fix?

Third, what are your gifts? What has God equipped you to do? What gifts would help you to carry out the calling? Where is the place that God has given you to exercise those gifts? What desires has He given you to exercise those gifts in particular?

Fourth, what is your internal sense of calling? What in your desires, dreams, or the voice of God motivates you to do something about the issue that is on your heart?

Fifth, what gifts do the people closest to you affirm that you have? Do others see the connection between the vision on your heart and the practical gifts that you have?

QUESTIONS TO CONSIDER:
1. What is your heart motivation in starting a new nonprofit?
2. Should I start a new nonprofit or partner with an existing nonprofit?
3. What is the need or problem in society that is on your heart?
4. What part has God played in inspiring your vision?

CHAPTER 2
LISTEN TO LEARN

"Most people do not listen with the intent to understand but with the intent to reply." ~ Steven Covey

Growing up, I loved to talk (and still do). My dad often told me that God gave us two ears and one mouth on purpose. It's because He wants us to listen more than we speak. Listening is one of the most vital skills to starting and leading a nonprofit organization. Oftentimes, we move too fast when we hear a call to a specific work. But we don't seek to understand the "what" of the calling. We are ready to do the work, but we are not prepared. We have not counted the cost of starting and leading a nonprofit. Neither do we have a clear understanding of the root of the problem that we are trying to solve. We only have solutions (we think) to the symptoms of the problem—and a heart to meet the need. We must learn to listen to God first, then seek wise counsel, and gain insight from key stakeholders concerning the real problem.

LISTENING TO THE STILL SMALL VOICE

I have learned in my journey that listening to God first provides insight into the unknown future. Just recently, one of my colleagues in a private foundation recommended that I partner with an established, reputable nonprofit to address a major issue in under-resourced communities around health disparities. I met with the CEO of the organization. We discussed our potential roles, benefits, and opportunities. We even discussed the value of working together. We agreed to pursue a major grant opportunity together that would provide more than $800K to the initiative.

When I returned home from the meeting, I prayed and asked God to reveal any reasons why Alliance for Greater Works™ should not partner with this organization. Later that evening, after a time in prayer and meditating on the Word of God, I begin to develop uneasiness in my thoughts about the partnership. I did not understand why at the time. But I have learned over the last thirteen years to always lead from the inside out. So the next day, I called the nonprofit executive at the organization and explained that I would not be partnering with them on the major grant project.

We ended the conversation pleasantly, and agreed that we would look for other opportunities to work together in the future. The large, established nonprofit pursued the grant opportunity, and was awarded a $500,000+ one-year grant for the programs and services they were going to provide to the community. After the grant award was announced, I began to doubt I made the correct decision by not partnering with that organization. But, five months later, the organization was portrayed negatively in the media for miscommunication and a lack of effectively leading the program. That was a situation that no one could have forecasted but God.

Listening to that still small voice is the sixth sense that you must have when leading. This voice must become your compass to your decisions. There will be moments when you want to go with the opportunity. But as an authentic leader, you must be willing to lead not based on what you see, but what you know from the inside.

Nehemiah sought God prior to asking the king for support in his endeavors. Prayer is not a substitute for work, but it is the preparation for success in your work. Prayer is that place of surrender, realizing that everything accomplished depends on God and His Word. Nehemiah prayed an extensive prayer starting in Nehemiah 1:5. In Nehemiah 1:11, he prayed, "...Lord, let your ear be attentive to the prayer of your servant, and to the prayer of your servants who delight to fear your name, and give success to your servant today, and grant him mercy in the sight of this man" (ESV).

Often we filter everything we hear through our own life experiences, and frame of reference. And consequently, a decision is made prematurely about the direction or priorities of the mission. God desires us to seek Him first and ask for His direction. He knows the beginning and the end, as well as the present and the future.

Many times, I've heard people say you don't need to pray for everything because some things are just common sense. I have learned through many lessons, that if I am doing this work for His Glory, then the answers and solutions for every situation will come from Him and not me. So my first priority is to listen to God. Because, it is through your listening you will know when to move, how to move, and even where to move.

Proverbs 19:20-21 says, "Listen to advice and accept instruction, that you may gain wisdom in the future. Many are the plans in the mind of a man, but it is the purpose of the Lord that will stand" (ESV). Take the time to listen and accept instruction from God so that you may gain wisdom in leading the future of your nonprofit. We often have a plan in our mind, but long-term success is linked to the God's purposes.

SEEK WISE COUNSEL

"Advice is like snow—the softer it falls, the longer it dwells upon, and the deeper it sinks into the mind." ~ Samuel Taylor Coleridge

Beyond hearing from God, starting and leading a nonprofit organization requires that you make wise business decisions—ensuring that the organization has a strong infrastructure that is necessary for success. For the visionary, often, our first paradigm shift is to realize that a nonprofit is a business. You, as the visionary of a new initiative, will be faced with the need to make calculated decisions each day in the journey to starting and leading the future of a 501(c)(3). Your leadership decisions impact not only the legal and business documents developed to establish the organization, but even the execution of the organization's programs and services to the community. There are long-term consequences to your leadership decisions that will affect the course of your nonprofit or ministry.

For example, when a leader decides to have questionable management or financial practices, it affects the credibility of the organization. In turn, that affects your ability to secure community support, including board leadership, volunteers, and financial supporters.

When I started Alliance for Greater Works™ thirteen years ago, I sought wise counsel. I started with individuals that I had relationship with in the business and nonprofit sector. They were able to provide insights into what I desired to do. I next researched similar nonprofits and entities, regionally and nationally, on the Internet. I developed a list of the organizations, their missions, and their programs and services. I then developed questions to ask the executive director of each organization to better understand their work. I emailed the leader first, introduced myself, my reason for contacting them and requested a 20- or 30-minute conversation with them to learn about their vision.

One hundred percent of the leaders welcomed my call and helped me to understand their mission and work, their lessons learned, and any recommendations for my journey. In addition, they provided insight and even asked questions of me that I could not answer. The questions required me to go back to the drawing board and better understand the need of the target audience I was called to serve.

Another place that I sought wise counsel was the funding community. My goal was to assess if organizations similar to the one I was starting had received funding. This helped me to explore and build relationships with potential funders and to identify other individuals or investors that might be interested in the type of mission being developed.

By listening and learning from the current nonprofit leaders and funding community, I was able to determine if the programs I envisioned were needed and if a new nonprofit was really necessary. Initially, I did not start a new nonprofit, but partnered with the Foundation for Community Empowerment to offer the training institutes. I strongly recommend identifying and partnering with an existing organization rather than creating a new nonprofit first if at all possible. The benefits of developing your program inside another organization can provide you the opportunity to learn, leverage the existing resources, and get hands-on experience.

The counsel leaders provided offered excellent insight. But I had to choose to act on the counsel. When visionary leaders are not willing to listen, learn, and choose to accept the insight we receive, we can delay our success.

Twenty years ago, I was selected to be part of a new leadership team to re-establish a nonprofit. The Texas attorney general's office had removed the founding executive director of the organization due to allegedly comingling and embezzling money. My role at the time was director of development. Each time I met with a potential donor—individual, corporation, or foundation—they reminded me of the past problems of the organization, and they all wanted to make sure the organization was really solid before supporting the mission again. Even though the organization's mission was greatly needed in the community, people would not endorse the mission because of previous leadership decisions. So, as a leader, it's important to know the legal, financial, and brand effects of your decisions.

Another source of wise counsel is reading nonprofit and for-profit business literature—books, blogs, and newsletters. Have your pulse on the state of the business world, the world of philanthropy and local, regional, and national news—it is all interconnected. I have developed many models as a result of reading an article, blog, or report that shares a for-profit model. As a result of reading something new, I was able to apply that model to my work or a nonprofit that I was working with. Reading is critical to the success of your organization.

GET INSIGHT FROM THE TARGET AUDIENCE

Finally, it is crucial that you assess your vision by talking with the target audience you desire to serve. This step will ensure that your nonprofit's mission is necessary and desired. When you don't listen to your target audience, your program results may become ineffective and utilize unnecessary resources.

While I was interviewing pastors to begin the work of Alliance for Greater Works™ in 2001, I saw the effects of not listening to key stakeholders firsthand.

A pastor shared a situation that occurred in his under-resourced community. He said that well-intentioned and resourced churches from other parts of the city came into his community to paint and repair boarded up houses, and beautify yards. They worked diligently, but the houses that the well-resourced churches were repairing were crack houses. The community boarded up the crack houses while the churches came and beautified the houses. So, basically, the well-resourced churches were encouraging the people on crack to stay in the community, while the churches and community leaders were trying to encourage them to leave the area or get help.

This situation occurred because the well-intentioned church did not seek first to listen and understand what the needs of the community were. They did not stop to connect with the current key stakeholders of the community, including churches, local organizations, and neighborhood leaders. The churches had a heart but did not stop to develop an opportunity to work collaboratively with the community to serve the community by understanding and coordinating the work.

WHAT DOES THE BIBLE SAY ABOUT WISE COUNSEL?

Counsel means advice, guidance, warning, alerting, suggestions, guidelines, and support. Wise means practical, prudent, shrewd, discernment, and insightful. The Bible speaks about wise counsel, when it says:

1. We need to trust in God vs. self: "Trust in the Lord with all your heart, and do not lean on your own understanding..." (Prov. 3:5; ESV). We can be misled by relying solely on our thinking. But by allowing God's thinking to become our thinking, we excel.
2. To be wise, counsel must come from "wise" sources: "Blessed is the man who walks not in the counsel of the wicked, nor stands in the way of sinners, nor sits in the seat of scoffers; but his delight is in the law of the Lord, and on his law he meditates day and night" (Psalm 1:1-2; ESV). Scripture is contrasted as a good source of counsel, as opposed to the counsel from people not worth listening to.
3. It is a sign of wisdom to listen to counsel: "The way of a fool is right in his own eyes, but a wise man listens to advice" (Prov. 12:15; ESV). Though we are not fools in the sense of rejecting God, we can act foolishly by not taking wise advice. It is a sign of wisdom when you ask others for advice.
4. Your thoughts may not be the source of the wisdom you need: "Whoever trusts in his own mind is a fool, but he who walks in wisdom will be delivered" (Prov. 28:26; ESV). To trust your own thinking and intellect is foolish, but the person who walks in the wise counsel of the Holy Spirit and wise men will be delivered.
5. Our counsel should come from many sources: "Without counsel plans fail, but with many advisers they succeed" (Prov. 15:22; ESV). There is provision and protection in the abundance of counselors. But when that wise direction or counsel is missing, leaders often fail and fall.
6. Take seriously the counsel you receive: "Keep hold of instruction; do not let go; guard her, for she is your life"

(Prov. 4:13; ESV). Rely on and hold strongly to direction and instruction. With wise instruction you will have life.
7. And, finally, Proverbs 20:18b says, "Plans are established by counsel..." (ESV). With wise counsel you will have a greater chance of success in implementing the vision God has given you.

QUESTIONS TO CONSIDER:
1. Have you taken time to pray and seek God's direction about the vision?
2. What is God's will regarding the work (the geographic location, the focus of the work, and how He would like you to accomplish it)?
3. Who do you need to seek wise counsel from: business persons, nonprofit leaders?
4. Have you listened to the concerns of members of the community you feel called to serve?

CHAPTER 3
LOOK AGAIN AND SEE THE NEED

"My destination is no longer a place, rather a new way of seeing."
~ Marcel Proust

Have you ever considered the difference between looking and seeing? I consider looking as passive or on the surface. For example, many times I have been guilty of looking at a person but really not seeing them, because I was focused on what was going on in my own world at the time. Meaning, I saw their body, but didn't take the time to look into their eyes. Perhaps, you too have looked at a person but did not see the pain in their eyes or the smile on their face. Or maybe, you asked them how they were doing, but you really didn't want to know or didn't expect them to tell you. Looking is like riding in a car, seeing people but not necessarily engaging with them. Not really taking the time to know them.

Seeing, on the other hand, speaks to understanding, insight, going deeper, discernment, and wisdom—seeing past facades, stereotypes, clichés and preconceptions. Oftentimes when I work with leaders and organizations, their brand in the community may look like they are well-run, systematic, and financially sound. But when I go deeper, I realize there are major dysfunctions, no systems in place, and the organization has a major financial deficit. On the other hand, I have worked with organizations that are not well known in the community. But when you look and see them at the core—they have great leadership, promising internal systems and controls, and a six-month financial reserve. Yet, the community at large doesn't really know them.

Do you see or only look at a situation? To "see" is to look past the obvious—the expected—and to take the time to find and perceive the root causes and not just what is seen on the surface. The first step in seeing the real needs of a community is facilitating a community assessment. A community assessment is a photo of the obscure assets and needs of a community. A community assessment provides a solid understanding of what the needs for services are, and who needs the programs. The community assessment process also helps the visionary refine their understanding of needs and assets. This improved understanding can be used to plan strategically and determine the desired outcomes and indicators for the program.

SEEING THE NEEDS

A clear understanding of the need of a community is necessary to effectively serve your target audience. You must be willing to look carefully and closely to see the real need. A need can be defined as the gap between what is and what should be. The community need can be felt by an individual, a group, or the entire community. It can be as concrete as the need for housing, food or water, or as abstract as improved community connectedness.

An example of a concrete need might be the need for fresh fruits and vegetables in a community where residents have to go out of their immediate neighborhoods to get healthy, reasonably-priced food products. More important to these same residents, however, might be a need to be valued for their knowledge, experience, and contributions to the community—an abstract need. Examining situations closely helps uncover what is needed and what will lead toward future improvements. Today, I often find that people really don't want to take the time to build relationships with the individuals and communities they want to serve. Trust me—my experience has taught me, it's critical.

There are many accounts in the Bible where a community assessment was utilized to get insight into a situation. One time was when the Lord instructed Moses to send twelve spies to explore Canaan, the land that God was giving the Israelites (see Numbers 13:1). When Moses sent the spies, he told them, "...Go up there into the Negev; then go up into the hill country. And see what the land is like, and whether the people who live in it are strong or weak, whether they are few or many. And how is the land in which they live, is it good or bad? And how are the cities in which they live, are they like open camps or with fortifications? 'And how is the land, is it fat or lean? Are there trees in it or not? Make an effort then to get some of the fruit of the land'" (NASB). The questions Moses asked were relevant to the place he was going. The key is to develop questions that will help you clearly understand the geographic area and the root cause of the problem you want to address.

Nehemiah also did a community assessment in preparation for rebuilding the walls of Jerusalem. He invested time, and made an estimated three-month journey from his home to Jerusalem. When Nehemiah arrived in Jerusalem, his number one priority was to survey the city. Nehemiah wanted to discover the size of the task, and to develop a plan for completion of the task. Nehemiah inspected the realities of the task God had given him to accomplish. This was not a causal or half-hearted survey—Nehemiah was very precise and thorough.

IDENTIFYING THE ASSETS

In addition to understanding the community needs, the assets of the community must be assessed and evaluated. Community assets are all the resources within a community that could potentially be used for the betterment of that community. Community assets fall into four categories:

1. GIFTS, SKILLS, AND CAPACITIES OF INDIVIDUALS.

Individuals are the basic building blocks of any ministry or community. Communities are stronger when there is high resident participation within the community. There are certainly challenges, since every individual has needs and deficiencies. However, it is also true that EVERY individual has gifts, capacities and abilities. Unfortunately few of these are being mobilized for community building purposes. Examples include the ability and interest in caring for children or the elderly, the ability to drive a van or bus, gifts in communication or teaching.

2. RESOURCES OF COMMUNITY-BASED NONPROFITS AND ASSOCIATIONS.

This is another category of community assets that are often overlooked. A powerful community is one in which all kinds of work is being done by local citizens united through associations. Examples of these types of organizations are neighborhood associations, PTA's, alumni associations, and church ministry groups, such as the women, men, or youth ministries.

3. RESOURCES OF LOCAL INSTITUTIONS.

Local institutions can represent significant concentrations of resources. They are often willing to allow their resources to be used for a variety of activities. Examples of institutions include churches, schools, hospitals, libraries, colleges, and universities.

4. PHYSICAL ASSETS AND NATURAL RESOURCES.

Every community has physical resources which could be more greatly used to build the community. Examples include parks, vacant lots, and abandoned buildings.

How does knowing about these assets benefit your vision to launch greater works? By discovering the community assets, you can then connect them to one another to form valuable relationships. You can also mobilize them to solve problems you are trying to address in your nonprofit ministry. The goal of this assessment is to activate and engage the assets. The purpose of this process is for you to first understand the community's own potential before looking for external resources. Ultimately, everyone in a community can be a force for community improvement if only we know and activate their assets.

By knowing and understanding the community assets, you will then be able to fully leverage the assets. The assets can be used as resources to improve the overall social issue while minimizing the amount of "new work" that you will launch. In short, the community assessment process helps the visionary refine his/her understanding of the needs and assets. This improved understanding can be used to engage partners, to plan strategically, and to determine the desired outcomes and indicators for the program.

WHICH APPROACH DO I TAKE?

We've all heard the expression, "Is the glass half empty or is it half full?" The answer to the question serves as an indicator of one's point of view. In other words, do you focus on what's missing or do you focus on what's there?

Traditional needs-based approaches to developing community programs focus on the needs, problems and deficiencies of a community. An example of this type of approach is government programs in which strategy only addresses the problem elements of a community, but neglects to build on the strength within the community.

As visionary, you must decide whether to take a traditional needs-based approach or an asset-based approach in your program design. The assets approach seeks to identify, mobilize and utilize a community's assets for the purpose of building the community. It asks, "What resources are present within the community?" instead of narrowly focusing on the needs, problems, and deficiencies in the community. This approach does not deny that there are problems, but chooses to build around assets instead of deficiencies.

ASSET APPROACH	NEEDS APPROACH
Seeks to mobilize individual gifts, skills, and capacities	Views individuals as clients with needs, problems, and deficiencies
Community-driven development	Development driven by external agencies or the "powers that be"
Relationship driven; dependent on collaborations, partnerships, and broad-based community participation	Dependent on one agency or a few individuals in the community who are designated as leaders
Identifies the community resource base before looking for external resources	Almost completely reliant on external resources, including volunteers, funding, and expertise

Recently Alliance for Greater Works™ was considering a collective impact strategy around formerly incarcerated mothers. After further investigation and talking to community stakeholders, we decided to change our strategy from needs-based to assets-based. We developed a strategy around mobilizing and engaging the skills, gifts, and capacities of all women in the targeted area verses focusing on only the formerly incarcerated mothers. By looking at the issue as half-full, we were able to implement a new, innovative strategy that not only engages formerly incarcerated women but all women of that community.

THE BENEFIT OF AN ASSET APPROACH IS THAT IT:

- Expands the community's vision of possibilities for itself;
- Taps wisdom within the community that is often overlooked;
- Improves community esteem, presents opportunities to use greater numbers of residents in development efforts;
- Increases the effectiveness and sustainability of community development efforts;
- Increases the attractiveness of community development efforts to outside funding sources;
- Increases the community's ability to identify its own economies and opportunities for residents;
- Further empowers the community to define its own agenda.

Mike Green in ABCD Principles lists twelve principles in support of the asset-based approach.[5] Mike states that, "Most communities address social and economic problems with only a small amount of their total ability. Much community capacity is not used and is greatly needed! This is the challenge and opportunity of community engagement. Everyone in a community has something to offer."

QUESTIONS TO CONSIDER:
1. What is the geographic area you will serve?
2. What are the needs in that community?
3. What are the assets—people, organizations, physical resources—in that community?
4. Will you position your nonprofit programs from a needs or asset approach?

CHAPTER 4
THINK DIFFERENTLY

A common definition for insanity is doing the same thing over and over again and expecting different results. The nonprofit sector is guilty of insanity. I find that there are many leaders with a passionate heart to change the world that start a new nonprofit, but the programs they create look the same as the current programs already developed in established nonprofits. We keep doing the same programs and delivering the same services in different organizations and getting the same results. Often results with limited success, or duplication of something implemented blocks away from our service area. So what is the solution?

Real transformation always starts in our thinking. Romans 12:2 tell us to be "...transformed by the renewing of your mind." To launch greater works that transform lives and communities, the founding leader and the start-up team must think differently about how they build the strategy of the new organization. By going through the process of researching national initiatives, learning what programs and services currently exist in the local community, seeking wise counsel and facilitating a community assessment, there should be a clearer understanding about the root cause of the problem you want to see change that should in turn help you to develop an effective strategy, a blue ocean strategy (I will define this shortly). Once you have your understanding, you'll be ready to determine your strategy and write a strategic plan.

WHAT IS STRATEGY?

Strategy is often misunderstood in the nonprofit sector. Oftentimes, founding leaders hire a consultant to create a strategic plan because a potential investor requires it or the founding leader knows they need to develop a plan. The document is written with the hopes of having a nonprofit strategy in place. However, the plan lands in a binder on the top shelf in an office collecting dust. Often, a visionary may not know what strategy is, why it is needed, or even how to use it.

Strategy gets its roots from the military, centering on setting objectives, gathering information (intelligence), and utilizing that information to make informed decisions about how to achieve a stated objective. The military strategy includes planning and executing a campaign, the movement and disposition of forces, and the deception of the enemy. Military strategy also involves using military resources such as people, equipment, and information against the opponent's resources to gain supremacy or reduce the opponent's will to fight, developed through the precepts of military science.[6]

In the business and nonprofit world strategy is more than an operational plan, budgeting, or conducting a feel-good retreat. It's more than writing a grant, conducting a building campaign, or creating a new program or a service. Whether in the for-profit or nonprofit world, strategy is not an option—it's essential to achieve greater works.

Strategy is about deciding what to do and what not to do in an organization based on a blend of facts and promising or best practices (the science) and a precision in creativity to adapt to an ever-changing environment (the art).[7] Strategy rests on a unique set of activities. It is the choice of activities and how they are performed that will lead to an organization's uniqueness. These activities have to reinforce one another.[8] They must bring a value and change in the lives of the customers.

Strategy is essentially about doing things different than other organizations in your community and achieving greater impact for the target audience. You must synthesize all the information gathered and determine the best path to achieving real social impact.

A BLUE OCEAN STRATEGY

One of the required readings during my Ken Blanchard Executive MBA program, that fast became my favorite book, was *Blue Ocean Strategy* by W. Kim, and R. Mauborgne. The book proposes a novel approach to creating groundbreaking strategies by envisioning the marketplace, whether business or nonprofit sector, as divided into blue oceans and red oceans.

In the red ocean, everything looks the same and limits are defined and accepted by all the entities in the ocean. It's over-crowded in the red ocean because the businesses imitate one another. The businesses operate in a status quo, comfortable environment. No innovation exists there and no organization really stands apart. I believe the red ocean is the color that it is because everyone is feeding off of one another. They are killing one another because the ocean is shrinking and stagnate, and there is no new life.

On the opposite side of the continuum, the blue ocean framework focuses on market distinction and innovation—it is un-crowded and beautiful in this ocean. In the blue ocean, entities thrive because they think outside of the box and implement inspiring and stretching program goals and organizations. They create uncontested market space and make similar businesses and organizations irrelevant through innovation.

The blue ocean strategy is a powerful concept that helps companies in their strategy formulation and in their obligations to reinvent themselves and find new markets. I imagine the blue ocean space as being vibrant, creative, and thriving. The businesses in the blue ocean are not stifled in their growth and have the ability to create a new way of doing business. The blue ocean offers unlimited growth opportunities, and the ocean is as far as they can see with no competitors in sight.

Finding a blue ocean doesn't necessarily require discovering a whole new service area, but rather looking at the problem to solve from an asset-based perspective verses a need-based perspective. This means that your programs are designed with a new way of thinking. An example of a successful blue ocean strategy is the Cirque du Soleil. The demand for traditional circuses was on the decline. Rather than ending the festival concept, they developed a strategy by thinking differently. They created an innovative strategy that includes the circus and theatre experience.

The nonprofit sector can learn lessons from this concept. The blue ocean strategy offers the social sector exciting oceans of opportunity for creating increased value at lower cost. The ocean becomes blue when nonprofits simultaneously achieve a leap in social good at lower costs by creating compelling and economically sustainable programs that stand apart. This occurs when leaders rethink their assumptions about community service by creating more impact for less effort. Nonprofits can no longer have good intentions and do things the same old way and lead to greater works. Neither can leaders any longer passionately create nonprofits with a red ocean mentality of simply filling the ocean with the same programs and services. We must think differently, lead differently, execute differently, and partner differently to achieve greater works. We must be willing to function with a blue ocean leadership point of view—when we do, all things are possible. The blue ocean is a way of thinking that leads to a strategy that allows the water to turn blue due to uniqueness of programs and services.

The nonprofit community must turn away from obsessing about the competition, and trying to be like another organization that appears to be great. Instead, nonprofits and ministries must turn toward their target audience and ask a set of basic questions, beginning with the issues of demographics, impact and reach.

1. Who is affected by this problem, facing it directly as a challenge?
2. How common or prevalent is the underlying condition or problem that the mission focuses on, for this demographic population?
3. How serious are the consequences for this not being met any better than it is now?
4. How much potential is there for addressing this with current expertise and in ways that could be applied now to affected communities and individuals?
5. How much potential is there to effectively create new approaches to address this with research? [9]

A blue ocean strategy asks us to focus on developing programs and services in creative ways that enrich lives in a way that no one else has thought of yet. We must be willing to shift the attention from short-term relief to bold goals that provide long-term solutions by tackling the root of social problems. Solving real problems and achieving greater works requires leaders not just to start a nonprofit, but sometimes to actually change the direction of the nonprofit sector by thinking differently.

CIRCLE OF SUPPORT

An example of a nonprofit blue ocean created is the one that I helped my first client develop for their organization—Circle of Support. Established in 1999, Circle of Support equips girls in South Dallas with the academic and life skills needed to become productive and responsible citizens. The nonprofit group was started by two professional women—Bernadette Nutall and Dianne Robison—who had a heart for the next generation of girls in under-resourced communities. They started their work as a mentoring program for elementary and middle school girls in the low-income neighborhood of South Dallas. The median household income in South Dallas is $15,000, the high school graduation rate is 42% and only 3% have a college degree (as compared to the Dallas average of 27%). Sixty-three percent of the households are single mothers, 54% of the residents are unemployed, and 42% do not own vehicles. The community has the highest rate with HIV positive/Aids in the area.

In 2001, the two ladies desired to create a blue ocean strategy for their organization that would position them as a unique organization. The strategy idea started when they attended a National Summer Learning Conference. This conference provides organizations the knowledge and tools to prevent student loss of knowledge and skills during the summer break. At this first conference, Bernadette and Dianne learned that more than half of the achievement gap between lower- and higher-income youth can be explained by unequal access to summer learning opportunities. Many low-income students lose at least one grade level between the end of a school year and the beginning of a new school year. As a result, low-income youth are less likely to graduate from high school or enter college. [10]

They also learned that children lose more than academic knowledge over the summer. Most children—particularly children at high risk of obesity—gain weight more rapidly when they are out of school during summer break. [11] This information changed the trajectory of their entire organization. The leaders and their board decided that they would position their organization as the premiere organization in the North Texas region to provide summer learning programs for the South Dallas area. The organization stopped administering after-school programs and focused solely on summer learning called Girl S.M.A.R.T. (Science, Math, Arts, Reading, and Technology). In 2007, the community insisted that the program also include boys.

Today, the Girl S.M.A.R.T. and S.M.A.R.T. Boys Summer Learning Program is the only comprehensive community program that targets the prevention of summer learning loss while providing support to working families by keeping children safe and healthy in South Dallas and surrounding communities. It is the only program that utilizes certified teachers, addresses the needs of the whole child, increases academic achievement, and enhances motivation and engagement in learning. The S.M.A.R.T. programs help develop and nurture new skills and talents but also help to improve self-esteem and confidence. The program has grown from 10 girls with a $5,000 budget to over 300 girls and boys from throughout the Dallas area with a nearly $500,000 budget. To learn more about Circle of Support and its work, go to www.circleofsupportdallas.org.

LINKING STRATEGY AND PROGRAM DESIGN AND OUTCOMES

Many new and small nonprofits find themselves struggling and scrambling due to limited financial resources even as community needs grow. Often times, those organizations are unsustainable and do not have capital because they do not have a clear program design and outcomes measures. They simply function by the seat of their pants. Strategy is important because it helps to direct your program design and outcomes.

To produce an effective nonprofit or ministry program with measureable outcomes, start with the process of creating a logic model. The purpose of the logic model is to provide you an at-a-glance road map outlining the order of events linking the need for the planned program with the program's desired results. Logic models are multi-faceted in their ability to assist leaders of nonprofits in program design, implementation, evaluation, and reporting results to funders. Logic models also assist you in writing your case for support and proposals.

A logic model is a visual, organized way to present and share your understanding of the relationships among the resources you have to operate your program, the activities you plan, and the changes or results you hope to achieve.[12]

Moreover, logic models can help demonstrate what additional resources are needed to achieve the goals of your program and what outcomes these resources can be expected to produce. The W.K. Kellogg Foundation has created a comprehensive guide for a logic model that gives you a step-by-step process.

Today, some funders will ask for a copy of your program logic model in evaluating grant proposals. The logic model process helps you to unpeel the layers of a spiritual and social problem and allow you to understand the exact area that you will focus your time, talents, and resources. By developing the logic model, you will be able to clearly understand your blue ocean strategy.

I can quickly identify those organizations that have not taken the time to do the critical work of creating a logic model. I know this because the programs are weak and ineffective, often a duplication of services. In addition, the programs and services are all over the place verses strategic and outcomes-driven. As a result, the program could quickly potentially fade into the abyss of the other U.S. 1.6 million nonprofits.

Below are the five key components required for the flow-chart logic model:

Planned Work describes the resources you think you need to implement your program and what you intend to do.
1. *Resources*—the human capital, financial, organizational, and community resources a program has available to direct toward doing the work.
2. *Program Activities*—are what the program does with the resources. Activities are the processes, tools, events, technology, and actions that are an intentional part of the program implementation. These interventions are used to bring about the intended program changes or results. Your intended results include all of the program's desired results (outputs, outcomes, and impact).
3. *Outputs*—are the direct products of program activities and may include types, levels and targets of services to be delivered by the program.

Your Intended Results include all of the program's desired results (outputs, out-comes, and impact).
4. *Outcomes*—are the specific changes in program participants' behavior, knowledge, skills, status and level of functioning.
    - Short-term outcomes should be attainable within one to three years,
    - Longer-term outcomes should be achievable within a four- to six-year timeframe.

5. *Impact*—is the fundamental intended or unintended change occurring in organizations, communities or systems as a result of program activities within seven to 10 years.[13]

WRITING A STRATEGIC PLAN

When the mission has been articulated, the critical issues identified, the strategy determined, and the logic model developed, the next step essentially involves putting all of that down on paper in a strategic plan. A strategic plan is a living document outlining the decisions and actions that shape and guide what your organization will be, what it does, and why it does it. The strategic planning process is viewed as the process of determining what an organization intends to be in the future and how it will get there. The strategic plan document includes:

- **Vision Statement**—an image of what success will look like. (We will discuss more in the next chapter.)
- **Mission Statement**—summarizes the "what, how, and why" of an organization's work.
- **Values**—the beliefs your organization holds in common and endeavors to put into practice. The values guide your organization in performing the work.
- **Statement of Faith** (if religious)—shared spiritual beliefs.
- **Target Audience(s) including geography**—a specific group of people within a target market that your programs and services are aimed at.
- **Goals and Objectives**—the plan of action. What the organization intends to do over the next three years. This will include program goals and outcomes.
- **Three-year Financial Budget**—Expressed in monetary terms, the board's and staff's decisions regarding how the organization will fulfill its stated purpose. The budget should include both income and expenses.

My hope is that you, the founding leader, will stop the insanity by thinking outside of the box to build a niche that creates a blue ocean strategy for your organization and in your program offerings.

EARNING BY LEARNING

The benefits of creating a strategic plan to direct the organization's future is evident in one of my current clients—Earning by Learning (EBL). Founded in 1996 by the Francis Rudine Family and Thelma Morris-Lindsey, founding director, EBL's mission is to empower children, strengthen schools, and foster literate communities through reading.

EBL is an evidence-based reading incentive model that is innovative in its approach and defies conventional wisdom. It is the fourth educational research program in the country with proven academic gain as touted by Harvard University's research findings. Since its inception the program has served more than 100,000 children in the Dallas area with an annual operating budget of less than $300,000.

The board leadership hired Alliance for Greater Works™ in 2012 to help the board and staff create a growth strategy plan to scale the reading incentive program to other school districts regionally and nationally while growing the annual operating budget and building their sustainability. Alliance for Greater Works™ consultant team and I worked with the board and staff over nine months to build EBL's new business model that includes an earned income strategy, an infrastructure strategy to increase staff and internal capacity, and a partnership strategy with Alliance for Greater Works™ and other organizations within the communities they serve.

Today, the organization has secured its first three-year independent school district client that provides EBL the opportunity to reach more than 2,000 new students in Richmond, VA and increase its operating budget to nearly $450,000 in the first year of the growth strategy. Earning by Learning's program model allows community stakeholders (investors) to see a return on their investment in children and reading while simultaneously giving children an opportunity to take ownership of their education. To learn more about Earning by Learning, go to www.eblofdallas.org.

QUESTIONS TO CONSIDER:

1. Answer the following questions to develop your blue ocean strategy:
    a. Who is affected by this problem, facing it directly as a challenge?
    b. How common or prevalent is the underlying condition

or problem that the mission focuses on, for this demographic population?
c. How serious are the consequences for this not being met any better than it is now?
d. How much potential is there for addressing this with current expertise and in ways that could be applied now to affected communities and individuals?
e. How much potential is there to effectively create new approaches to address this with research?

2. Develop your first logic model. Start with the outcomes and impact section.
3. Write a draft of your strategic plan.

CHAPTER 5
LEAD WITH A VOICE OF VISION

"You can speak well if your tongue can deliver the message of your heart."
~ John Ford
"Vision is the art of seeing the invisible" ~ Jonathan Swift

When a founding leader understands the heart of the matter, listens to learns, sees the root cause verses the symptoms of human suffering, and thinks differently in how to position his/her nonprofit and program strategy—they are ready to focus their energy on developing and leading with a compelling vision.

The chief responsibility of a leader is to cast the vision so that people can grasp it and run with it. Leaders are not the hands of the work. They are the head that sets the direction, communicates what needs to be done, inspires trust and motivates others to execute the plans. Vision communicates to those inside and outside the organization the end goal for the nonprofit's existence.

THE POWER OF VISION

Management author, Tom Peters, identifies a clear vision of the desired future state of the organization as an essential component of high performance. Widely-read organizational development author, Warren Bennis, identifies a handful of traits that made great leaders great. Among them is the ability to create a vision. So, what is a vision and how do you get one?

A vision is a *guiding image of success formed in terms of a contribution to society*. A vision is the ultimate goal you are pursuing. It is a picture or visual of the ideal future. The vision is the "artist's rendering" of the achievement of the organization. It is a description, in words, that conjures up a similar picture for each member of the group, of the destination of the group's work together.

You will never be greater than the vision that guides you. The vision statement should require the organization's members to stretch their expectations, aspirations, and performance. Without a powerful, attractive, valuable vision—why bother?

Dr. Martin Luther King, Jr. said, "I have a dream," and what followed was a vision that changed a nation. That famous speech is a dramatic example of the power that can be generated by a person who communicates a compelling vision of the future. He described a world where his children "will not be judged by the color of their skin but by the content of their character." He created powerful images resulting from the values of a love for mankind, respect, and freedom for all—values that resonate with the founding values of the United States. Today, King's vision continues to mobilize and guide people beyond his lifetime, because it clarifies a significant purpose, provides a picture of the future, and describes values that resonate with people's hopes and dreams.[14]

Some visions also include a reason to address the problem and a timeframe to accomplish the vision. Vision builds trust, collaboration, interdependence, motivation, and mutual responsibility for success.[15] It's something to reach for and it creates hope and sets expectations. Vision starts in the heart, moves to the mind, and then becomes the voice of the visionary leader. If it's compelling enough, it can inspire and motivate the entire world.

When we are called to carry out a God-inspired vision, we must be prepared to share the vision with others. In the book of Nehemiah, the vision was to rebuild the walls of the city. When it was time for Nehemiah to communicate the vision, he shared it first with the king to ask for permission to leave his position and request resources to rebuild the wall. In Nehemiah 2, Nehemiah gives us a model of how to lead with a voice of vision when communicating to others.

VISION MUST HAVE PASSION

The first element in leading with a voice of vision is passion. Passion describes a powerful range of emotions including love, joy, excitement, pain, or brokenness. A leader must have passion to communicate the vision effectively. When leaders don't have passion for the vision, it is evident—they are viewed as low energy, no excitement, burnt out, or even lethargic.

As a visionary leader, you must be passionate about the condition you want to see changed. Without passion, the message will feel sterile or just a lot of words without real meaning. With passion, the vision will be stimulating and inspiring. Nelson Mandela lived with passion for his vision of a South Africa without apartheid. His actions and message was cohesive. He said, "During my lifetime I have dedicated myself to this struggle of the African people. I have fought against white domination, and I have fought against black domination. I have cherished the ideal of a democratic and free society in which all persons live together in harmony and with equal opportunities. It is an ideal which I hope to live for and to achieve. But if needs be, it is an ideal for which I am prepared to die" (Nelson Mandela). Do you have enough passion that you are willing to die for your vision?

Nehemiah was full of passion. He had spent nearly four months weeping, praying, and fasting about the vision. As I said before, he risked his job and his life by entering the king's presence with a sad face. Nehemiah had enough passion for his vision he was willing to risk his life to share that vision.

COMMUNICATE THE VISION AS A SOLUTION

A compelling vision provides a solution to a problem. When Nehemiah traveled to Jerusalem, he had to share his vision with the people of Jerusalem. He had not interacted with the people prior to this time, so I imagine he no idea how they would respond. Nehemiah had to speak with inspiration, clarity, and conviction because the people had lived among the broken-down walls of the city for more than a century. There were many potential responses the people could give Nehemiah when he shared the vision to rebuild the wall. They could run him out of town, laugh at him, criticize him, try to harm him, or simply ignore him.

In Nehemiah 2:17-18, Nehemiah spoke with a voice of vision by personalizing the message to show that he and the citizens were on the same team. He said, "You see the bad situation we are in, that Jerusalem is desolate and its gates burned by fire. Come, let us rebuild the wall of Jerusalem that we may no longer be a reproach" (NASB). Then he told them about how the gracious hand of God had been on him, and about his conversation with the king. It's important when you are sharing the vision to share your connection to the problem. In this case, it was Nehemiah's homeland and God had burdened him with this vision.

STATE THE PROBLEM

Nehemiah began communicating the problem first. "You see the bad situation we are in, that Jerusalem is desolate and its gates burned by fire" (Neh. 2:17; NASB). By stating the problem, it answered the question of the purpose for the vision. It clarifies exactly what is trying to be accomplished and the purpose of the new nonprofit or program.

When I read this scripture the very first time, I found it interesting that Nehemiah first told the people about the walls being broken. Wasn't that an insult to their intelligence? They already knew the condition of the walls. But, sometimes we become so comfortable with our current situation that we forget that it's not normal. After a century of living in a certain state or condition, the problem stops being a problem, becoming instead a way of life. For the people in Jerusalem, it was a norm for them to not have the walls around their city. Maybe some of them had never experienced the walls around their city. For them, this was all they knew.

But Nehemiah knew this was not normal. The walls were important because they protected the city. As the visionary, when we can help people to see the world again through fresh eyes it changes their perspective and dreams. The people of Jerusalem had lost sight of what could be and should be. They had to see the problem through Nehemiah's eyes in order to realize it was a problem that could be solved.

All of us have been in a situation that is a problem, but nothing is done until someone brings it to our attention. Maybe it's being comfortable with a job that pays the bills, but you have grown out of. Or maybe it's living with an unhealthy body that is out of shape. Vision always challenges us to see past what we've come to see as normal, to see what could be and should be.

PROPOSE A SOLUTION

The third component of a compelling vision is to offer a solution. "Come, let us rebuild the wall of Jerusalem" (Neh. 2:17; NASB). The solution is obvious, but it took one person to be bold enough to verbalize it and lead the people to action. Nehemiah communicated exactly what God was calling him to do and spoke with a voice of vision—"Let's rebuild the wall." Solutions always inspire possibilities and a paradigm shift. When the people heard Nehemiah speak the vision with passion, I can imagine them saying, you know Nehemiah is right we need to rebuild the wall. We can do this! When we speak with a voice of vision, we unlock the power and potential of people to think and see differently. A clear and compelling vision will include a solution to a problem.

WHAT IS THE WHY BEHIND THE WHAT?

Nehemiah's vision included another essential component—the reason why it was important to solve the problem. Nehemiah said, "Come, let us rebuild the wall of Jerusalem that we may no longer be a reproach" (Neh. 2:17; NASB). Nehemiah knew that the walls were an insult to the residents of the city, but even worse, they were an insult to God. God's reputation was at stake. This was supposed to be God's city, but the Ark of the Covenant was missing, sacrifices had ceased, and the glory was gone. Nehemiah gave them a compelling reason to rebuild the walls: for God's glory and their good.

THE TIMING IS RIGHT

The walls had been in ruins for years. Why did Nehemiah believe the timing was right? Nehemiah 2:18 says, "And I told them how the hand of my God had been favorable to me, and also about the king's words which he had spoken to me" (NASB). Nehemiah's vision stated that now is the time to rebuild because of God's sovereign orchestrating the circumstances. God had groomed Nehemiah to be ready for the dream when it came. All of Nehemiah's life had been ordered by the Lord to bring him to this time, this place, and for this very special purpose. God himself was on the move to rebuild those walls.

It's an exciting thing to realize that God is on the move. The people came in agreement with God and Nehemiah and the work began. Nehemiah 2:18 says, "Then they said, 'Let us arise and build.' So they put their hands to the good work" (NASB). People desire to be led with vision and when a leader can clearly and concisely articulate it—people are ready to respond.

Once you've clearly defined your vision and shared it, your organization and program activities, the activities of your employees and the resources of your nonprofit should be in alignment with the vision. Vision helps people make smart choices, because their decisions are being made with the end result in mind. As goals are accomplished, the answer to "What next?" becomes clear. Vision allows us to act from a proactive stance, moving toward what we want rather than reactively away from what we don't want. Vision empowers and excites us to launch and reach for greater works.

QUESTIONS TO CONSIDER:

1. Review your vision. Is it clear and concise?
2. Can you articulate it succinctly with passion?
3. How do you know when is the right time to unveil the vision?

NEXT STEPS AND RESOURCES TO LAUNCHING GREATER WORKS™

"Life's most persistent and urgent question is, 'What are you doing for others?'" ~ Martin Luther King, Jr.

I hope this book motivates and inspires you to pursue your God-inspired vision of launching a new program strategy or nonprofit organization. Understand that this work is not easy nor does it happen in a short period of time. It is a journey. Are you ready to move forward, obedient to the call? Or will you let your negative thoughts talk you out of pursuing something greater in your life? Perhaps, with your current work schedule and personal commitments, you don't feel you have time to even answer the questions at the end of each chapter. Or, the process feels overwhelming, and you're not sure you have the stamina to make it happen.

Let me suggest some next steps to get you started in launching your vision.

First: Don't allow your racing thoughts to stress you out. Take it slow. I recommend that you start this journey by spending dedicated time in solitude, praying and seeking God for direction—a weekend, 21 or 40 days. Flip through this book again to review the key points and use it as a resource.

Second: Find two other individuals that will serve as your truth-tellers. You will desperately need people who will speak truth to you and will hold you accountable as you move through this process. These individuals could eventually become the founding board members if your idea becomes a 501(c)(3). I don't recommend choosing relatives if you plan to select them as board members.

Third: Write down the thoughts, ideas, and conversations that you have during your time with God and other individuals. Keeping a journal is important as you walk out this journey. Review your notes periodically to encourage yourself.

Fourth: Consider, researching and partnering with an existing nonprofit to develop your program or service instead of starting a new nonprofit. The benefits of developing your program inside another organization can provide you the opportunity to learn the nonprofit sector and key stakeholders, leverage community resources, and get hands-on experience.

CHECKLIST OF ESSENTIALS TO LAUNCH A 501(C)(3) NONPROFIT:

- Instruction manual for daily reading and living—the Holy Bible;
- Two or three truth-tellers, who will keep you focused and moving in the right direction;
- Journal to record the triumphs, challenges, and lessons learned that will help you to remember and pass along to others;
- Hire a coach or consultant to walk you through the process of launching a nonprofit or ministry. Alliance for Greater Works™ offers these services.

OTHER HELPFUL ONLINE DOCUMENTS:

- Download the community assessment template; *http://www.acf.hhs.gov/programs/ocs/resource/conducting-a-community-assessment-1*
- Download the logic model from W.K. Kellogg Foundation; *http://www.wkkf.org/resource-directory/resource/2006/02/wk-kellogg-foundation-logic-model-development-guide*

PART 3
OVERVIEW

THERE ARE WAYS THAT I CAN HELP YOU IN LAUNCHING OR GROWING YOUR 501(C)(3) NONPROFIT, CONTACT:

Alliance for Greater Works™
Voice: (817) 835.0271
Website: www.allianceforgreaterworks.org

Alliance for Greater Works™ is a 501(c)(3) nonprofit that unlocks the power and potential of nonprofit leaders, organizations, and investors working together to multiply impact and transform communities.

Since 2001, we have increased the ability of over 7,500 mission-driven leaders and organizations through training and strategic consulting services.

WE HELP NONPROFITS AND COMMUNITIES BY:
- Building a new generation of leadership;
- Developing and implementing action plans to grow their impact and financial resources;
- Placing them on a path to sustainability;
- Communicating their value to diverse groups of generous givers and funders;
- Connecting them to other parts of the community.

WE HELP INVESTORS PUT THEIR MONEY WHERE THE IMPACT IS BY:
- Developing, executing, and monitoring a strategy and plan;
- Identifying organizations to partner with;
- Assessing the impact of current or potential grantees;
- Working collaboratively to help organizations improve their effectiveness and sustainable results.

ABOUT THE AUTHOR

Sherrye Willis is the founder and CEO of Alliance for Greater Works™. Sherrye has more than 25 years' experience in the nonprofit sector, serving on both sides of philanthropy including executive director of a private family foundation and a chief development officer in major higher education and art institutions.

She has consulted and coached in numerous sectors for hundreds of organizations, including Dr. Tony Evans' National Church-Adopt-A-School Initiative, Center for Philanthropy Bermuda, Concord Church, Esping Family Foundation, Foundation for Community Empowerment, Dallas Leadership Foundation, and Builders of Hope Community Development Corporation.

Willis has also presented to local, state, national, and international audiences as a keynote speaker, trainer, and facilitator in the areas of leadership, board development, change management, faith-based community/economic development, framework of poverty, fundraising, grant writing, collaboration models and more.

In 2012, Sherrye was one of 150 U. S. leaders invited to the White House to discuss challenges facing local communities. The goal was to learn from pioneers who are driving change in challenging times and to explore new ways federal policymaking can support their endeavors. Only three Texas organizations were invited.

In 2003, Sherrye authored and designed the first Texas capacity building program called Building Capacity, Building Communities program funded by the Compassion Capital Demonstration Fund Program. The purpose of the program was to help faith-based and community groups build capacity and improve their ability to provide social services to those in need.

Sherrye has a MBA from Grand Canyon University and BBA from Northwood University. She is married to her best friend, Joe for twenty-five years. Joe and Sherrye are members of New Life Fellowship, Arlington, TX where they serve as global missions leaders.

ENDNOTES

1. Blanchard, K. and Hodges, P., The Servant Leader (2003) Thomas Nelson, Inc.

2. Blanchard, K. and Hodges, P., The Servant Leader (2003) Thomas Nelson, Inc.

3. Adapted from Bryson's Strategic Planning in Public and Nonprofit Organizations.

4. *http://www.merriam-webster.com/dictionary/heart*

5. ABCD principles by Mike Green, ABCD Training Group.

6. School of Advanced Air and Space Studies.

7. Porter, M., What is Strategy? (1996) Harvard Business Review

8. Porter, M., What is Strategy? (1996) Harvard Business Review

9. Platt, T. 2010, *http://plattperspective.wordpress.com/2010/01/11/nonprofits-and-blue-ocean-strategies*

10. *National Summer Learning Association (2013) http://www.summerlearning.org/?page=know_the_facts*

11. National Summer Learning Association (2013) http://www.summerlearning.org/?page=know_the_facts

12. W.K. Kellogg Foundation, 2006.

13. Adapted from the W.K. Kellogg Foundation Logic Model Guide, 2004.

14. Blanchard, K. (2007). Blanchard Management Corporation Publishing as Prentice Hall.

15. Blanchard, K. (2007). Blanchard Management Corporation Publishing as Prentice Hall.